Language Handbook Worksheets
Additional Practice in Grammar, Usage, and Mechanics

*Correlated to Rules in the Language Handbook
in the Student Edition*

HOLT, RINEHART AND WINSTON

A Harcourt Education Company

Orlando • **Austin** • New York • San Diego • Toronto • London

Staff Credits

Associate Director: Mescal Evler

Manager of Editorial Operations: Robert R. Hoyt

Managing Editor: Bill Wahlgren

Project Editor: Katie Vignery

Component Editors: Marcia Kelley, Karen H. Kolar, James Hynes

Editorial Staff: *Associate Editors,* Kathryn Rogers, Christopher LeCluyse; *Assistant Managing Editor,* Mandy Beard; *Copyediting Supervisor,* Michael Neibergall; *Senior Copyeditor,* Mary Malone; *Copyeditors,* Joel Bourgeois, Jeffrey T. Holt, Suzi A. Hunn, Jane Kominek, Désirée Reid; *Editorial Coordinators,* Marie H. Price, Robert Littlefield, Mark Holland, Jill Chertudi, Tracy DeMont, Marcus Johnson; *Support Staff,* Pat Stover, Matthew Villalobos; *Word Processors,* Ruth Hooker, Margaret Sanchez, Kelly Keeley, Elizabeth Butler

Permissions: Tamara A. Blanken

Design: *Art Director, Book Design,* Richard Metzger; *Design Manager, Book & Media Design,* Joe Melomo

Prepress Production: Beth Prevelige, Simira Davis

Manufacturing Coordinator: Michael Roche

Printed in the United States of America

ISBN 0-03-073921-7

12 13   179   09 08

TABLE OF CONTENTS

LANGUAGE HANDBOOK 1
THE PARTS OF SPEECH

LANGUAGE HANDBOOK 2
AGREEMENT

LANGUAGE HANDBOOK 3
USING VERBS

LANGUAGE HANDBOOK 4
USING PRONOUNS

LANGUAGE HANDBOOK 5
USING MODIFIERS

LANGUAGE HANDBOOK 6
PHRASES

LANGUAGE HANDBOOK 10
WRITING EFFECTIVE SENTENCES

LANGUAGE HANDBOOK 11
CAPITALIZATION

LANGUAGE HANDBOOK 12
PUNCTUATION

LANGUAGE HANDBOOK 13
PUNCTUATION

LANGUAGE HANDBOOK 14
PUNCTUATION

LANGUAGE HANDBOOK 15
SPELLING

LANGUAGE HANDBOOK 16
GLOSSARY OF USAGE

This booklet, *Language Handbook Worksheets,* contains practice and reinforcement copying masters that cover the material presented in the Language Handbook section of *Elements of Literature, Third Course.* The rules cited in the head of each worksheet correspond directly to the grammar, usage, and mechanics rules and instruction covered in the Language Handbook. Tests at the end of each section can be used either for assessment or as end-of-section reviews.

A separate ***Answer Key*** for the *Language Handbook Worksheets* provides answers or suggested responses to all items in this booklet.

LANGUAGE HANDBOOK **1** **THE PARTS OF SPEECH**

| WORSHEET 1 | **Identifying Nouns**

EXERCISE A Underline all of the nouns in the following paragraph. If a noun appears more than once, underline it each time it appears.

> **EXAMPLE** [1] <u>Craters</u> formed by <u>meteorites</u> have shallow <u>floors</u> and uplifted <u>centers</u>.

[1] Mercury is the planet nearest the sun. [2] Recently, data from spacecraft have shown astronomers that Mercury, like our Moon, is covered with craters. [3] The surface of Venus may also be cratered, but thick clouds of gas hide the landscape from telescopes. [4] Craters are formed when large meteorites, which are fragments of comets or asteroids, collide with a planet or a planet's satellite. [5] Some of the craters on the Moon are 320 miles wide.

EXERCISE B Underline all of the nouns in the following paragraphs. If a noun appears more than once, underline it each time it appears.

> **EXAMPLE** [1] The <u>islands</u> of <u>Hawaii</u> consist of <u>lava</u> and <u>ash</u> built up from the <u>floor</u> of the <u>ocean</u>.

[1] The formation of a volcanic island is a remarkable process. [2] This process often occurs over millions of years. [3] Erupting volcanoes build mountains on the floor of the sea. [4] Each eruption adds more lava to the pile of volcanic rock until, after many years, the volcanic mountain comes within reach of the waves. [5] The submerged island sometimes becomes a coral reef. [6] Other islands rise high above the surface of the ocean, forming rugged mountains with ridges, canyons, and cliffs.

[7] Plants and animals come to the island, either blown in on the wind or washed in with the current. [8] Some forms of life travel to the new island on natural rafts of tree limbs and matted vegetation. [9] Other organisms are carried by the birds that come to the island from other lands. [10] On the Galápagos Islands some forms of life, such as tortoises and sunflowers, grow much larger than they do on the mainland.

WORKSHEET 2 | Identifying and Using Pronouns

EXERCISE A   Each of the following sentences contains two pronouns. Circle each pronoun, and draw an arrow to the noun for which it stands.

EXAMPLE **1.** Mr. Platero owns two dogs, (which)(he) adopted from the animal shelter.

1. Roberto passed the ball to Elena, who caught it easily.

2. Otis called his sister, but she didn't answer.

3. When asked about the game, Mike said, "I didn't see it."

4. Since Gabriella found the money, the cash belongs to her unless it is claimed.

5. The children said they like the new bus driver who wears the blue hat.

6. Although Elliot studied French in school, he didn't feel comfortable speaking it.

7. Denise brought sandwiches with her on the hike and carried them in a knapsack.

8. "I," Jerry said, "surprised myself."

9. Because Sheila enjoyed musical comedies, she tried to see them as often as possible.

10. Keiko enjoyed volleyball so much she played it every day after school.

EXERCISE B   In the following paragraph, fill in the blanks with pronouns that refer to the italicized nouns.

EXAMPLES Any *nurse* [1] __who__ served in a Red Cross hospital
during World War I risked [2] __her__ life.

Edith Cavell was a British *nurse* [1] _____ served in Belgium during World War I.

In 1907, *Dr. Antoine Depage* had asked Miss Cavell to come to Brussels. [2] _____

wanted [3] _____ *hospital* modernized according to the principles of Florence

Nightingale. After the outbreak of the war in 1914, [4] _____ became a Red Cross

hospital. The Germans marched into *Belgium,* although [5] _____ was a neutral

country. The hospital was filled with many casualties of the war. Edith Cavell joined an

underground *group* [6] _____ gave aid to Belgians of military age and to escaped

Allied prisoners. The *Germans* discovered the group, and in 1915 [7] _____

arrested Edith Cavell and thirty-four other members. *Edith Cavell,* because of

[8] _____ religious convictions, refused to lie, even in order to protect

[9] _____. [10] _____ lost her life to a firing squad on October 12, 1915.

LANGUAGE HANDBOOK 1 THE PARTS OF SPEECH

WORKSHEET 3 | Identifying Adjectives

EXERCISE A   Underline each adjective in the following paragraph. Do not include the articles *a, an,* and *the.*

> **EXAMPLE** [1] Bonsai is the art of growing <u>tiny</u> trees.

[1] In Japan, some people grow miniature trees that have a famous history and an important place in horticultural art. [2] Through pruning and fertilization, the trees are trained to keep the shape and proportion of larger trees. [3] The trees often have small leaves and small fruit. [4] The trees have an old and wind-swept appearance, as though they had grown in the outdoors. [5] With bonsai, gardeners can create realistic landscapes in pots and carry scenes of mountain crags or vast plains into their homes.

EXERCISE B   Underline each of the twenty-five adjectives in the following story, and draw an arrow from the adjective to the word or words it modifies. Treat hyphenated compound words like *spine-tingling* as one word. Do not include the articles *a, an,* and *the.*

> **EXAMPLE** <u>Scary</u> stories can make the imagination run wild.

On hot summer nights, Julio and the other boys sleep out in the yard. They put up a tent in a dark corner, where the trees and bushes are thick. That way the boys can easily imagine they are in wild, uninhabited country.

One evening Mike suggested that they tell ghost stories or tales of bear hunts. After a particularly spine-tingling story, Mike couldn't sleep; he was too nervous.

About midnight he saw something move in the shadows. "Yeow!" he cried out. "There is a big bear! It is really huge!"

In the sudden confusion, the small tent collapsed on top of the boys; each one seemed eager to go in a different direction. Anxious parents ran out of the nearby house. They found a coal-black dog. Like a bear, this animal was very curious. It was sniffing at the tangle of arms, legs, and bodies under the tent.

LANGUAGE HANDBOOK 1 — THE PARTS OF SPEECH

WORKSHEET 4 | Identifying and Using Verbs

EXERCISE A   Underline each verb in the following paragraph. There are twenty-five of them, and all are action verbs. There may be several verbs in a sentence.

> **EXAMPLE** [1] The art group carefully <u>planned</u> and <u>built</u> a small clubhouse.

[1] Mark, Louisa, and Djuana formed an art group. [2] Since they needed a clubhouse, they planned the construction of a small geodesic dome. [3] The group financed the structure through the sale of some of their work. [4] Louisa sold a portrait and an abstract painting. [5] Mark constructed a Tiffany-style lamp, and the Posnicks quickly bought it and placed it in their brownstone apartment across the street. [6] Djuana sketched several local scenes, carved the sketches into linoleum blocks, made greeting cards with the blocks, and sold the cards through a local novelty store. [7] The group carefully studied *The Whole Earth Catalog* for instructions. [8] Louisa, Mark, and Djuana decided on a 10 1/2- × 8-foot building. [9] Louisa, the math whiz, performed the necessary mathematical calculations. [10] Mark, an expert bargain finder, shopped for the materials. [11] With the group's earnings, he purchased wood struts, spoke hubs, and plastic covering. [12] The group asked Mark's parents for the use of part of their back yard. [13] They started the construction work on Monday. [14] Louisa cut the wood to the necessary dimensions. [15] Mark formed the cut wood into triangles, and Djuana fastened the triangles together in the shape of a dome. [16] They finished the skeletal structure on Friday. [17] On Saturday they attached the plastic covering. [18] That evening the group celebrated its success in the new clubhouse.

EXERCISE B   The following items contain nouns modified by adjectives. Construct a sentence with each group of words by supplying verbs to link the nouns and adjectives, and write the new sentences on the lines provided. Use five different linking verbs.

> **EXAMPLE 1.** the stormy weather *The weather looks stormy.*

1. the dull knife _____

2. the haunted house _____

3. the shy child _____

4. the calm lake _____

5. the bitter medicine _____

LANGUAGE HANDBOOK **1** **THE PARTS OF SPEECH**

| WORKSHEET 5 | Using and Identifying Helping Verbs

EXERCISE A   Complete the following sentences by writing suitable helping verbs on the lines provided. Then, circle the entire verb phrase.

EXAMPLE   **1.**   __(Did)__   the teacher (explain)?

1. _____ you ever seen a Kabuki play?

2. His car _____ going too fast for safety.

3. I _____ waiting for Helen.

4. _____ you met my mother?

5. It _____ be later than you think.

6. Edena _____ becoming an excellent soccer player.

7. If he _____ read better, he _____ learn more.

8. There _____ been serious consequences.

9. Mr. Prinz _____ not _____ persuaded to change.

10. _____ you read "For My People" by Margaret Walker?

EXERCISE B   Each sentence in the following passage contains at least one verb phrase. For each verb phrase, underline the helping verb(s) once and the main verb twice.

EXAMPLE   [1] How many elements <u>does</u> air <u>contain</u>?

[1] Since no one can see the air, some people in the past did not consider it real. [2] The ancient Greek philosopher Anaximenes, however, did not agree with these people. [3] He believed that air must be one of the foundations of all matter.

[4] One evening Anaximenes was walking in the moonlight. [5] While looking up at the sky, he must have seen a rainbow made by the moon. [6] Unlike other Greeks, he did not believe that the rainbow was a goddess. [7] He was not surprised to see the rainbow because he believed that it was made by the effect of light on compressed air.

[8] Like Anaximenes, we must admit that the air does contain something real. [9] Scientists have found nitrogen, oxygen, and other elements in the air. [10] We may discover new facts about air now that we are investigating other planets.

LANGUAGE
HANDBOOK **1** **THE PARTS OF SPEECH**

| WORSHEET 6 | Identifying and Using Adverbs

EXERCISE A Circle the adverb in each item. Then, draw an arrow to the verb it modifies. On the line provided, state whether the adverb tells *how, when, where,* or *to what extent.*

> EXAMPLE ___when___ **1.** The big drawing (always) attracts a crowd at the county fair.

_____ **1.** For weeks merchants cheerfully gave numbered tickets with purchases.

_____ **2.** My cousin Lorraine and I finally collected forty tickets.

_____ **3.** "If we're lucky," I often told Lorraine, "we will win that camping equipment."

_____ **4.** Saturday came, and we eagerly waded through the crowd at the fair.

_____ **5.** The rules stated that the holders of winning tickets must be there.

_____ **6.** Promptly at midnight, they started the drawing.

_____ **7.** "The winner of the camping gear is 608–1313!" shouted the announcer. "Will the holder of number 608–1313 come here?"

_____ **8.** Lorraine's success completely surprised everybody.

_____ **9.** She walked to the platform slowly for her prize.

_____ **10.** She exclaimed, "This is the first prize I have ever won!"

EXERCISE B Modify each verb in the following paragraph by filling in each blank with an appropriate adverb. Choose varied, interesting adverbs.

> EXAMPLE [1] Several of the drama students rehearsed _together_ to prepare for the auditions.

Rena [1] _____ wanted to get a part in her school's production of *The Diary of Anne Frank.* She was [2] _____ nervous about auditioning, and she [3] _____ awaited the day for tryouts. To prepare herself, she [4] _____ scanned the play over the weekend. [5] _____ she went back and [6] _____ studied the role of Anne. [7] _____ she began to understand how it must have felt to live in hiding for so long. She wondered if she could [8] _____ portray the girl who had [9] _____ written the diary.

Continued ☞

Rena arrived in the auditorium [10] _____. [11] _____ she looked, she saw other students [12] _____ thumbing through scripts. She [13] _____ watched the first group of students read a scene. [14] _____ her turn came. She [15] _____ hoped that her understanding of the character would come through in her reading. As she began to read the part, she relaxed [16] _____. She [17] _____ enjoyed bringing the play to life.

After her turn, she [18] _____ returned to her seat. She sat [19] _____ waiting to hear the drama teacher's decision. She smiled [20] _____ when she heard the teacher say, "The role of Anne Frank— Rena Ross."

EXERCISE C On the lines provided, revise each of the following sentences by adding at least one appropriate adverb. Try not to use the adverbs *too, so,* and *very*.

> EXAMPLE **1.** Computer science degrees are popular because job opportunities in that field are good. *Computer science degrees are quite popular because job opportunities in that field are exceedingly good.*

1. First, Antonio took the screen door off its hinges; then, he removed the torn screen and replaced it with new material. _____

_____

2. Kyle returned the reference book to Tonya, but she had planned her report without it.

_____

_____

3. The sun rose, hot and bright, but as the day progressed, dark clouds began to appear.

_____

_____

4. Ruth typed her research report on the computer, but she didn't remember to save the document. _____

_____

5. When Yusef was picking out new glasses, he told the salesperson that he wanted wire frames. _____

_____

LANGUAGE HANDBOOK **1** **THE PARTS OF SPEECH**

WORKSHEET 7 | **Identifying Adverbs**

EXERCISE A   Each of the following sentences contains an adverb in italics. Draw an arrow from the adverb to the word it modifies. On the line provided, tell whether the modified word is a verb, an adjective, or an adverb.

EXAMPLES   _adjective_   **1.** We saw a *very* uplifting movie.

_____verb_____   **2.** Luis *usually* plays right field.

_____   **1.** Ms. Katz plays tennis *well*.

_____   **2.** Henry Louis Gates, Jr., is an *exceptionally* talented writer.

_____   **3.** Melba *seldom* loses her head.

_____   **4.** Herbert seemed *unusually* happy.

_____   **5.** Should I slice the ancho chilies *now*?

_____   **6.** Tranh cried out, "Don't run *so* fast!"

_____   **7.** I *always* enjoy Gary Soto's poetry.

_____   **8.** A *rather* funny clown was juggling oranges.

_____   **9.** "I'm *too* drowsy for words," Annette yawned.

_____   **10.** Sue works *unusually* hard on Saturdays.

_____   **11.** Fran answered *somewhat* enthusiastically.

_____   **12.** Does hay *actually* cause hay fever?

_____   **13.** They play an *extremely* fast game.

_____   **14.** We will play a double-header *tomorrow*.

_____   **15.** At formal occasions, Jake speaks *properly*.

_____   **16.** The *dangerously* narrow bridge scared me.

_____   **17.** Can you *really* capture chiggers alive?

_____   **18.** The second speech was *less* interesting.

_____   **19.** He was *fully* aware of his plight.

_____   **20.** Florence *occasionally* eats sushi.

Continued ☞

EXERCISE B Underline each adverb in the following sentences. Then, circle the word or words the adverb modifies. On the line provided, write whether the adverb tells *how, when, where,* or *to what extent.*

EXAMPLE _____*when*_____ 1. (Shall) we (leave) now?

_____ **1.** Akio arrived early.

_____ **2.** I can run faster than you.

_____ **3.** Lim Sing seems very sure of herself.

_____ **4.** Later I believed him.

_____ **5.** Our soccer team was too slow.

_____ **6.** Is he always early?

_____ **7.** Did you know that your new books are here?

_____ **8.** Did you work hard?

_____ **9.** Marina has been there.

_____ **10.** This math problem is especially hard.

_____ **11.** The boys work slowly.

_____ **12.** Well, what shall we do now?

_____ **13.** This Incan pottery was expertly made.

_____ **14.** She will never believe you.

_____ **15.** If you need any help, I will be there.

_____ **16.** Emilia danced gracefully.

_____ **17.** After saying goodbye to his mother, Joshua left yesterday for school.

_____ **18.** She learned to make tamales easily.

_____ **19.** Carla often goes to jazz concerts.

_____ **20.** The fandango dance troupe rehearsed diligently.

_____ **21.** The rain pounded heavily on the skylights and ran over the tops of the gutters.

_____ **22.** Merrilee had soon finished washing the windows, so she polished the mirrors.

_____ **23.** Will you please get the dog, which is digging in the back yard, and bring it here?

_____ **24.** Kirk next diced onions and green peppers and put them into the pot to simmer.

_____ **25.** The bowl and the beaters used for beating egg whites must be completely free of grease.

LANGUAGE HANDBOOK 1 THE PARTS OF SPEECH

WORKSHEET 8 | Identifying and Using Prepositions, Adverbs, Conjunctions, and Interjections

EXERCISE A   Each of the following sentences contains two prepositions. Draw a line under each preposition.

> **EXAMPLE** **1.** The books <u>of</u> poetry are <u>on</u> the top shelf.

1. Do your work in study hall or do it at home.

2. After the dance we went to Gerry's house.

3. Lorraine Hansberry's plays about racial and social issues were praised by critics.

4. Behind the fence I found my bicycle, with a flat tire.

5. Since September she has been the principal of our school.

6. As I walked from the building, I met the principal on the steps.

7. For social studies I read a book about Sacajawea.

8. Margaret lives in an apartment building on Sheridan Avenue.

9. Beyond the valley the mountains were black against the sky.

10. During vacation Derrick kept busy working around the house.

EXERCISE B   On the line provided, classify the italicized word in each sentence as a preposition or as an adverb. Use the abbreviations *PREP* for preposition and *ADV* for adverb.

> **EXAMPLES** __PREP__ **1.** Leroy jumped *across* the creek.
>
> __ADV__ **2.** Can you make it *across*?

_____ **1.** Time passes *on* and waits for no one.

_____ **2.** Shawn put his trophy *on* the coffee table.

_____ **3.** "Have you seen Mr. Bluehouse *since*?" she asked.

_____ **4.** "I haven't seen him *since* the party," I replied.

_____ **5.** *Behind* me stood Coach Davis.

_____ **6.** There is a good restaurant *up* the road about three miles.

_____ **7.** Marshall went *back* for help.

_____ **8.** The rescue team quickly headed *under* the bridge.

_____ **9.** We were just sitting *down* when the phone rang.

_____ **10.** Please put the cat *out* before you go.

Continued ☞

EXERCISE C   On the lines provided, write short sentences using the italicized words as directed.

> **EXAMPLE** **1.** *behind* as a preposition   *The bowls were behind the plates.*

1. *up* as a preposition _____

2. *up* as an adverb _____

3. *down* as a preposition _____

4. *down* as an adverb _____

5. *over* as an adverb _____

EXERCISE D   Underline the conjunction or conjunctions in each sentence.

> **EXAMPLES** **1.** I recognized you <u>but</u> not your brother.
>
> **2.** <u>Neither</u> Sam <u>nor</u> Luisa has arrived yet.

1. Every day I have to feed both my dog and my cat.

2. The crowd roared when Antoan hit the home run.

3. Always try to do the job quietly and correctly.

4. The clown looked sad but made me laugh.

5. Let me know if you want to borrow that Rudolfo Anaya novel.

6. Since they gave me tickets, I plan to go.

7. I can ride my bicycle on the road or through the woods.

8. "Slow but sure" is my motto.

9. The defendant could either pay a fine or go to jail.

10. I enjoy the writings of both James Baldwin and Ralph Ellison.

EXERCISE E   Underline the interjection in each sentence.

> **EXAMPLE** **1.** <u>Oh</u>, never mind.

1. Whew, I'm glad that test is over.

2. I wonder if this plate is hot—yikes!

3. I've seen that movie, oh, four or five times.

4. Look, I don't think I can make it to the party.

5. After reading *Romeo and Juliet,* Carla said, "Wow, what a great play!"

| WORSHEET 9 | **Reviewing the Parts of Speech** |

EXERCISE On the line provided, write the part of speech of each italicized word. In making your decision, ask yourself how the word functions in the sentence.

EXAMPLES __*verb*__ **1.** They often *study* math together.

__*noun*__ **2.** Ms. Shapiro has a large desk in her *study*.

_____ **1.** Kimiko took an express *train*.

_____ **2.** A *train* whistle sounded in the distance.

_____ **3.** I will *train* your dog.

_____ **4.** *Cross* the street on a green light.

_____ **5.** Turn right at the next *cross* street.

_____ **6.** She was wearing a gold *cross*.

_____ **7.** The boss will *fire* me.

_____ **8.** The *fire* department is always ready.

_____ **9.** We saw a large *fire* in the distance.

_____ **10.** He has a bald *head*.

_____ **11.** Who is the *head* usher?

_____ **12.** Isabel will *head* the freshman class.

_____ **13.** Botan can *field* a ball faster than any other player.

_____ **14.** The new athletic *field* is ready for use.

_____ **15.** A *field* mouse scampered by.

_____ **16.** Everyone *left* the building in a hurry.

_____ **17.** I sat on the *left* side of the room.

_____ **18.** Turn *left* at the next corner.

_____ **19.** Let's walk *around*.

_____ **20.** Diego and Brian walked *around* the block.

_____ **21.** What did she *say* to you?

_____ **22.** *Say*, watch out for that tree.

_____ **23.** We decided to go *inside* after we ate.

_____ **24.** One of the Russian dolls was hidden *inside* the other.

_____ **25.** *Hey*, where are you going?

LANGUAGE HANDBOOK **1** **THE PARTS OF SPEECH**

WORKSHEET 10 Test

EXERCISE A Above each italicized word, write the part of speech of the word. Use the abbreviations *N* for noun, *PRON* for pronoun, and *ADJ* for adjective.

                                     ADJ   N   N

        EXAMPLE [1] Listening is an important *social skill* with many *benefits*.

[1] *Ernest, who* is invited nearly everywhere by *friends,* has his *favorite definition* of "life of the party." [2] *He* believes that a person can be in the *limelight* merely by being a *good* listener. [3] "*People* at a *party,*" he says, "welcome a *chance* to make a *big* impression. [4] If you are *quiet* and listen attentively, *you* give them an opportunity to make a *grand display* of their *talents.* [5] If you let *other* people impress you, *they* will be impressed by your *graciousness.*"

EXERCISE B On the lines provided, write complete sentences using the italicized words as directed.

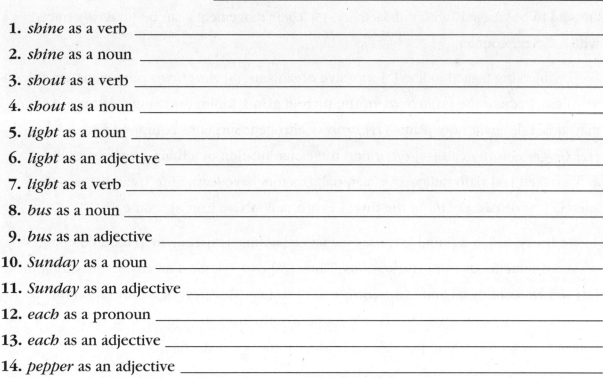

        EXAMPLE **1.** *picture* as a verb *Can you picture yourself as a wildlife researcher?*

1. *shine* as a verb _____

2. *shine* as a noun _____

3. *shout* as a verb _____

4. *shout* as a noun _____

5. *light* as a noun _____

6. *light* as an adjective _____

7. *light* as a verb _____

8. *bus* as a noun _____

9. *bus* as an adjective _____

10. *Sunday* as a noun _____

11. *Sunday* as an adjective _____

12. *each* as a pronoun _____

13. *each* as an adjective _____

14. *pepper* as an adjective _____

Continued ☞

15. *pepper* as a verb _____

16. *pepper* as a noun _____

17. *bicycle* as a noun _____

18. *bicycle* as an adjective _____

19. *mushroom* as a noun _____

20. *mushroom* as a verb _____

EXERCISE C   Above each of the twenty-five words in italics in the following paragraph, write the part of speech of the word. Use the abbreviations *N* for noun, *PRON* for pronoun, *ADJ* for adjective, *V* for verb, *ADV* for adverb, *PREP* for preposition, and *CONJ* for conjunction. Study the way the word is used before making up your mind.

                                     V   ADJ
EXAMPLES   Atoms [1] *form* the building blocks of all the [2] *chemical* elements.

The destructive [1] *force* of the atom is familiar to all of us, but we know [2] *considerably* less about the atom's constructive uses. Materials [3] *like* sulfur, zinc, [4] *and* iodine can be made radioactive for scientific purposes. The atoms of such materials are said to be "tagged" with radioactivity. [5] *Their* movements can be [6] *easily* traced with a Geiger counter.

By injecting tagged iodine [7] *into* live organisms, [8] *American* physicians are able to learn much about the [9] *activity* of the thyroid gland. Biologists using [10] *tagged* atoms may at last discover how plants [11] *process* nitrogen. Surgeons equipped with a [12] *Geiger counter* can [13] *often* find the exact location of a brain tumor by tracing a dye mixed [14] *with* radioactive material. Doctors have learned to treat diseases like anemia [15] *or* cancer [16] *of* the thyroid with radioactive iron or iodine.

Industry, too, has found [17] *uses* for tagged atoms. [18] *They* help food companies preserve some foods from [19] *spoiling*. They [20] *can* also be a means of measuring the [21] *thickness* of metal and [22] *plastic*, and of testing the effect of motor oil on the [23] *durability* of car engines. [24] *Undoubtedly*, the uses for tagged atoms will continue to grow, making possible [25] *future* miracles of science.

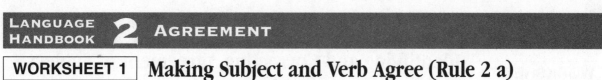

LANGUAGE
HANDBOOK 2 AGREEMENT

| WORKSHEET 1 | Making Subject and Verb Agree (Rule 2 a)

EXERCISE A On the line provided for each of the following subjects and verbs, write *S* if the verb is singular or *P* if the verb is plural.

EXAMPLES ___*S*___ 1. she falls

___*P*___ 2. they talk

_____ 1. Bill walks   _____ 11. Sarah takes

_____ 2. he tries   _____ 12. we go

_____ 3. I make   _____ 13. people give

_____ 4. Jim wishes   _____ 14. you leave

_____ 5. she has   _____ 15. Luis carries

_____ 6. cats are   _____ 16. birds fly

_____ 7. classes have   _____ 17. there it goes

_____ 8. it was   _____ 18. teams lose

_____ 9. stars shine   _____ 19. reporters ask

_____ 10. the dog lies   _____ 20. it exists

EXERCISE B Some of the subjects and verbs paired in the following items agree in number; some do not agree in number. If an item is incorrect, draw a line through the verb and write the correct form on the line provided. If an item is already correct, write *C*.

EXAMPLES ___*C*___ 1. Tyrone gives

___*writes*___ 2. woman ~~write~~

_____ 1. planes fly   _____ 11. houses has

_____ 2. pupils thinks   _____ 12. man drink

_____ 3. motor runs   _____ 13. mountains stands

_____ 4. cities is   _____ 14. guard waits

_____ 5. child ask   _____ 15. cats jump

_____ 6. player have   _____ 16. dentist advise

_____ 7. horse looks   _____ 17. people was

_____ 8. tree grows   _____ 18. Liz give

_____ 9. flowers are   _____ 19. desk sits

_____ 10. dresses seems   _____ 20. girls risk

LANGUAGE
HANDBOOK **2** AGREEMENT

WORSHEET 2 | **Identifying and Correcting Agreement of Subject and Verb (Rules 2 a–f)**

EXERCISE A   In each of the following sentences, circle the subject and then underline the verb form in parentheses that agrees with the subject.

> **EXAMPLE   1.** (One) of the paper cups (*was*, *were*) leaking.

1. Cosmic rays in this room (*is, are*) striking us right now.

2. The cause of her troubles (*seem, seems*) apparent.

3. Each of you (*has, have*) heard this legend.

4. Neither of the girls (*own, owns*) a bicycle.

5. Everyone in my class (*knows, know*) that!

6. The fibers of the wood (*is, are*) then crushed.

7. Neither Kendra nor Susan (*plays, play*) the piano.

8. A few of your friends (*were, was*) here.

9. The length of these boats (*are, is*) twenty feet.

10. One of these notebooks (*belongs, belong*) to you.

EXERCISE B   In the following sentences, draw a line through each verb that does not agree with its subject and write the correct verb form on the line provided. If a sentence is already correct, write *C*.

> **EXAMPLE** _____is_____ **1.** Neither of the reports ~~are~~ clearly written.

_____ **1.** Several of the students has written reports on the Chinese poet Li Po.

_____ **2.** Some of Li Po's poems imitates the rhythms of folk songs.

_____ **3.** Some of the team members have played professionally.

_____ **4.** Not one of the bills were counterfeit.

_____ **5.** Both of the sentences say the same thing.

_____ **6.** A few of the band members was not in uniform.

_____ **7.** Neither of the rugs lie flat.

_____ **8.** Every one of these planes carries fifty passengers.

_____ **9.** Either the students or the teacher know the answer to that.

_____ **10.** All of the supplies in the boxes were bought at the supermarket.

WORKSHEET 3	# Using Correct Agreement with Subject and Verb (Rules 2 a–f)

EXERCISE A   In the following sentences, draw a line through each verb that does not agree with its subject, and write the correct verb form on the line provided. If a sentence is already correct, write *C*.

EXAMPLE ___are___ 1. Ms. Ogata and her class ~~is~~ taking a field trip.

_____ 1. Both the cha-cha and the rumba are Cuban dances.

_____ 2. Either nachos or celery were served with the guacamole.

_____ 3. Arturo or Beatrice always lead our class discussions.

_____ 4. Either Nuna or Rosalinda are going to meet us.

_____ 5. Have either Andrea or Edna spoken to you?

_____ 6. The winner and new champion is Lynn Contrucci!

_____ 7. Neither the players nor the coach were surprised by the win.

_____ 8. Red beans and rice is a popular Saturday night meal.

_____ 9. Pang and Jamyce probably has the directions.

_____ 10. Either the director or the stagehands usually arrives first.

EXERCISE B   In the following sentences, circle the subject and underline the verb form in parentheses that agrees with the subject. *Note:* Some subjects are compound.

EXAMPLE 1. (One) of the most popular literary forms (*is, are*) the mystery story.

1. The first mysteries in English (*was, were*) written by Wilkie Collins.

2. *The Moonstone,* the most successful of Collins's novels, (*was, were*) written in 1868.

3. Its characters and plot (*fascinates, fascinate*) readers.

4. Edgar Allan Poe, author of short stories, poems, and essays, (*is, are*) credited with developing the character of the modern detective.

5. The detective in the stories of Arthur Conan Doyle, Sherlock Holmes, (*solve, solves*) mysteries by using deduction.

6. Agatha Christie and Dorothy Sayers (*is, are*) two other popular mystery writers.

7. Either Hercule Poirot or Miss Marple (*sniffs, sniff*) out the clues in Christie's novels.

8. Neither suspense nor surprise (*is, are*) lacking in any of Christie's works.

9. Many of Walter Mosley's books (*features, feature*) private eye Easy Rawlins.

10. The title of each of Sue Grafton's novels, which feature the detective Kinsey Millhone, (*begin, begins*) with a letter of the alphabet.

WORKSHEET 4   **Other Problems in Subject-Verb Agreement (Rules 2 a, b, g, i, k–m)**

EXERCISE   Circle the subject in each of the following sentences. Then, underline the verb in parentheses that agrees with the subject.

> EXAMPLE 1. The (news) of the president's illness (<u>*was*</u>, *were*) a shock to many people.

1. Fortunately, his injury (*doesn't, don't*) look too serious.

2. My birthday gift from Uncle Cesar (*was, were*) two books by Rudolfo Anaya.

3. About three quarters of the book (*focus, focuses*) on modern artists from Latin America.

4. *Harlem Shadows* (*is, are*) considered one of Claude McKay's most important works.

5. Sports (*was, were*) one of the topics of discussion at lunch yesterday.

6. The scissors (*is, are*) lying on the counter next to the sink.

7. "Strange Legacies" (*is, are*) a poem by Sterling A. Brown.

8. Two hours (*is, are*) enough time to spend on this math homework.

9. The swans floating on the sparkling lake (*turn, turns*) to look at me.

10. Doughnuts (*doesn't, don't*) make a very nutritious breakfast.

11. The most peaceful time of his life (*was, were*) his early childhood days.

12. Hot Springs, Arkansas, (*attracts, attract*) more than five million visitors every year.

13. Two thirds of the stolen bicycles (*has, have*) been recovered.

14. Richard (*doesn't, don't*) like to play tennis or racquetball.

15. Statistics (*seem, seems*) to be my sister's most challenging course this semester.

16. The gloves (*was, were*) a gift from my best friend, Maria.

17. Gloria (*doesn't, don't*) mind helping with the decorations for the dance.

18. The Saint Elias Mountains (*stand, stands*) along the southeastern border of Alaska.

19. The Knights of Pythias (*performs, perform*) charitable work such as supporting children's homes and summer camps.

20. Thirty dollars (*is, are*) a lot to pay just to see a basketball game.

21. Two of the magazines (*arrive, arrives*) worn and crumpled.

22. Measles (*causes, cause*) a pink rash all over the body.

23. *Rewards* (*is, are*) a colorful collage by Phoebe Beasley.

24. These balloons (*doesn't, don't*) have enough helium in them.

25. Those petunias (*is, are*) a colorful addition to the landscaping in front of the library.

LANGUAGE HANDBOOK 2 AGREEMENT

WORSHEET 5 | Identifying Agreement with Collective Nouns and with Subjects That Follow Verbs (Rules 2 h–j)

EXERCISE A In each of the following sentences, underline the correct verb form or contraction in parentheses.

> EXAMPLE **1.** (*Here's*, *Here are*) the missing engine part.

1. (*Where's*, *Where are*) Sara and Julia?
2. Here (*is*, *are*) the girls.
3. There (*is*, *are*) numbers on all the parts to be cleaned.
4. (*Here's*, *Here are*) some more parts that must be numbered.
5. (*Where's*, *Where are*) that yellow chalk?
6. Where (*is*, *are*) the gasoline and clean rags?
7. (*There's*, *There are*) rags on that shelf.
8. Where (*is*, *are*) the bolt that fits here?
9. (*There's*, *There are*) no numbers on these cleaned parts!
10. (*Here's*, *Here are*) the reason.

EXERCISE B In each of the following sentences, underline the correct verb form in parentheses.

> EXAMPLE **1.** The International Club (*meet*, *meets*) once a month.

1. A squadron of navy planes (*fly*, *flies*) overhead.
2. Our herd of Ayrshire cattle (*is*, *are*) the largest in the state.
3. The class (*run*, *runs*) to their seats when the bell rings.
4. The flock of wild geese flying above us (*were*, *was*) a beautiful sight.
5. Behind closed doors the jury (*were*, *was*) deliberating.
6. The committee (*was*, *were*) encouraged by our consideration of its offer.
7. The faculty (*doesn't*, *don't*) agree with one another.
8. The audience (*have*, *has*) given two standing ovations for Sweet Honey in the Rock.
9. What (*has*, *have*) the team done to improve their skills this year?
10. A group of students (*discuss*, *discusses*) a story by Ron Arias.

LANGUAGE HANDBOOK 2 AGREEMENT

WORKSHEET 6 | **Reviewing Agreement of Subject and Verb (Rules 2 a–j)**

EXERCISE A   In each of the following sentences, circle the subject and underline the verb form in parentheses that agrees with the subject.

> **EXAMPLE 1.** (Both) of those buildings (*was, <u>were</u>*) designed by I. M. Pei.

1. (*Where's, Where are*) the hammer or the ax?

2. Neither Kenneth nor Geraldine (*dance, dances*).

3. (*Has, Have*) anyone sampled moussaka and other Greek dishes?

4. This collection of poems (*look, looks*) interesting.

5. The crowd (*was, were*) angrily shouting at one another.

6. (*There's, There are*) only twelve students in the class.

7. Each of those jackets (*costs, cost*) too much.

8. Bread and butter (*is, are*) a fattening combination.

9. Both of the meals (*look, looks*) good.

10. The rash on her hands (*is, are*) probably poison ivy.

11. Kathy, along with her sister, (*has, have*) chicken pox.

12. (*Where's, Where are*) Malcolm or Maria?

13. Every one of the actors (*needs, need*) another rehearsal.

14. After their defeat the team (*was, were*) wearing gloomy expressions.

15. (*Is, Are*) Quentin or Bea going to type my paper?

16. A ring of towering mountain peaks (*enclose, encloses*) the valley.

17. Jack or Isaac (*wake, wakes*) up usually before anyone else.

18. Most of the exhibit (*features, feature*) works by Cuban sculptors such as Juan Jose Sicre..

19. (*Here's, Here are*) the bulbs for that light fixture.

20. Some of the poems in that collection (*is, are*) by Al Young.

21. The committee head, not the staff or the volunteers, (*is, are*) responsible.

22. Everything that you have given me to do (*has, have*) been completed.

23. (*Was, Were*) even a few of the poetry readings well done?

24. Either Armando or Brigit (*accompany, accompanies*) Paul on the piano.

25. Why (*don't, doesn't*) Janelle or Maria open the door to the cafeteria?

Continued ☞

Elements of Literature

EXERCISE B   In the following sentences, draw a line through each verb that does not agree with its subject and write the correct verb form on the line provided. If a sentence is already correct, write *C.*

EXAMPLES ____*C*____ **1.** Several Japanese silk weavings are hanging in the museum.

____*wants*____ **2.** Neither Gary nor Hector ~~want~~ to leave yet.

_____ **1.** Two songs by Gloria Estefan is included on that CD.

_____ **2.** Does Al or Fern know why radium glows in the dark?

_____ **3.** The reporters on our newspaper belongs to the Newspaper Guild.

_____ **4.** There are both tin and steel in a tin can.

_____ **5.** My science class has been experimenting with dry ice.

_____ **6.** Each of them have seen a fly's eyes through a magnifying glass.

_____ **7.** Everyone in the class was to give a report.

_____ **8.** There's two sides to that question.

_____ **9.** Have either Teresa or Vera ever told you that story?

_____ **10.** Some of us has been studying electricity.

_____ **11.** Both of my sisters want to be dog trainers.

_____ **12.** Several of his friends enjoys reggae music.

_____ **13.** Where's those tickets to the Keb' Mo' concert?

_____ **14.** Some of my friends take gymnastics lessons.

_____ **15.** Does macaroni and cheese make a good supper?

_____ **16.** How was the main dish and dessert today?

_____ **17.** The cut of her clothes are always just right.

_____ **18.** Both Susan and Bernardo play a good game.

_____ **19.** All of the tea were cold already.

_____ **20.** Do either of them know the way home?

_____ **21.** The main attraction are outstanding television advertisements.

_____ **22.** Thirty dollars is entirely too much to pay for a dinner for two.

_____ **23.** The Philippines are located in the southwest Pacific Ocean.

_____ **24.** Is the scissors in the top kitchen drawer or out in the garage?

_____ **25.** The organization known as the Daughters of the American Revolution promote good citizenship.

WORKSHEET 7 ## Making Pronouns Agree with Their Antecedents (Rules 2 n–q)

EXERCISE A   In the following sentences, some of the pronouns and their antecedents are in italics. Draw a line through each italicized pronoun that does not agree with its antecedent, and write the correct pronoun above it. Not every sentence has an error.

its
EXAMPLE 1. *One* of the buildings lost ~~*their*~~ roof during the tornado.

1. If you see *either* of my sisters, ask *them* to call me.

2. *Anybody* in the first group may present *his or her* report now.

3. *Neither* of the boys has completed *their* paper on Cornel West.

4. *Everyone* wore *their* costume to the party.

5. Not *one* of the books was missing *their* cover.

6. *Each* of the dogs was looking for *its* trainer.

7. *Anyone* who thought that deserved what *they* got.

8. *Neither* of the girls would lend me *their* book.

9. *Everybody* should accept *their* responsibilities.

'10. *Nobody* on the girls' softball team forgot *their* mitt.

EXERCISE B   Fill in the blank in each of the following sentences with a pronoun or a pair of pronouns that agrees with its antecedent(s). Circle the antecedent(s).

EXAMPLES 1. (Everyone) brought *his or her* skates.

              2. Only (one) of the girls brought ___*her*___ tennis racket.

1. Many of the parents voiced _____ opinions.

2. No one wanted _____ name mentioned in the paper.

3. Each student was given a locker for _____ equipment.

4. If everyone had _____ way, we'd never get anything done.

5. Both Mrs. Larson and Mr. Feldman took _____ classes on a trip.

6. Everybody said what _____ thought.

7. Neither Juan nor Steve wanted to have _____ picture taken.

8. Some of the group expressed _____ opinions quite frankly.

9. Both the carpenter and the welder finished _____ work yesterday.

10. A person should be careful in _____ usage of English.

LANGUAGE HANDBOOK **2** AGREEMENT

WORKSHEET 8 | Ensuring Pronoun-Antecedent Agreement (Rules 2 p–r)

EXERCISE A   On the line provided in each of the following sentences, write the pronoun or pronouns that agree with the antecedent.

> **EXAMPLE 1.** Neither Shada nor Ellie has really perfected ___*her*___ backhand.

1. Either Don or Thomas will write _____ report on the origins of classical music.

2. Ramona and Angelo have finished _____ sketches and will begin painting tomorrow.

3. Kareem and Steven both want to do _____ how-to speeches on kite making.

4. Either Dinah or Terri left _____ keys lying on the bench.

5. The coach and the team captains picked up _____ clipboards and called the team together.

6. Daniel and his brother rode _____ bikes to the Earth Day celebration.

7. Either Philip or Ryan will display _____ sculptures at the local art gallery.

8. Has she or her sister memorized _____ part for the play?

9. Either Christina or Julia said that Dan Namingha is _____ favorite painter.

10. Mr. Stamos and Ms. Hirota are helping _____ students prepare for the science fair.

EXERCISE B   On the line provided in each of the following sentences, write the pronoun or pronouns that agree with the antecedent.

> **EXAMPLE 1.** The students who rode ___*their*___ bikes to the game arrived late.

1. Clayton is someone who sets _____ goals high and never backs away from a challenge.

2. The younger cat, which tends to devour _____ food too fast, has been put on a special feeding schedule.

3. Hattie McDaniel, who won an Oscar for _____ performance in *Gone with the Wind,* was the first African American to win an Academy Award.

4. Any student who comes up with _____ own original topic should get Mr. Chuen to approve it.

5. Elena, who wrote _____ history paper on Filipino immigration after World War II, could probably answer your question.

LANGUAGE HANDBOOK **2** **AGREEMENT**

WORKSHEET 9 **Test (Rules 2 a–r)**

EXERCISE A In each of the following sentences, circle the subject(s) and underline the verb form in parentheses that agrees with the subject(s).

> **EXAMPLE 1.** (*Does, Do*) (anybody) know the seven wonders of the ancient world?

1. There (*is, are*) only one wonder that still stands.

2. Everyone in Egypt (*know, knows*) about the ancient pyramid of Khufu.

3. Either Earline or Helga (*say, says*) that four huge cathedrals could fit inside this pyramid.

4. How many of the wonders (*was, were*) destroyed by earthquakes?

5. One of the wonders (*was, were*) sold for scrap metal.

6. Jeremy and Angelo (*is, are*) building a model of the Hanging Gardens of Babylon.

7. A committee (*decide, decides*) on seven new wonders.

8. Anyone with a suggestion (*has, have*) the right to submit it.

9. Many tall buildings in this country (*is, are*) being considered.

10. There (*is, are*) many modern creations that would qualify.

EXERCISE B Circle the antecedent(s) in each sentence. Then, underline the correct pronoun in parentheses.

> **EXAMPLE 1.** (Everyone) there offered (*his or her, their*) help.

1. Nan and Aretha bought (*her, their*) own tickets.

2. She or Sally will lend you (*her, their*) books.

3. One of the men forgot to bring (*his, their*) tools.

4. The captain of the women's basketball team brought (*her, their*) own coin to the coin toss.

5. Each new student has a guide assigned to (*him or her, them*).

6. Both of the girls had (*her, their*) notes handy.

7. Neither of the boys finished (*his, their*) job.

8. All citizens should accept (*his or her, their*) responsibilities.

9. Few boys on the cricket team did (*their, his*) best.

10. Anybody can learn to play mah-jongg if (*he or she, they*) will concentrate.

Continued ☞

LANGUAGE HANDBOOK 2 WORSHEET 9 (continued)

EXERCISE C   In the following sentences, draw a line through each incorrect verb or pronoun and write the correct form on the line provided. If a sentence is already correct, write *C.*

EXAMPLES   ___*C*___ **1.** Neither of the boys played his best game.

___*his*___ **2.** One of the boys lost ~~their~~ money.

_____ **1.** A person is always pleased when others laugh at their jokes.

_____ **2.** Neither of the children know how to swim.

_____ **3.** Each of Lynn Whitfield's roles is demanding.

_____ **4.** Ask Lisa and Francesca for their opinions.

_____ **5.** Only a brave person would risk their life in such a heavy sea.

_____ **6.** The trial of the three suspects has been postponed.

_____ **7.** Neither John nor Bob had gotten their hair cut.

_____ **8.** I think nobody could do this job by themselves.

_____ **9.** Some of the motorists want a change in the driving laws.

_____ **10.** Here's some ballots that have not been counted.

_____ **11.** Bread and bagels was not on the same aisle of the grocery store.

_____ **12.** Each of her grandparents live alone.

_____ **13.** One of her daughters looks exactly like her.

_____ **14.** Both women, when challenged, showed their true character.

_____ **15.** Every one of the games were close.

_____ **16.** Anybody can build their own boat with this kit.

_____ **17.** Do either Carmen or Barika have a driver's license?

_____ **18.** The bottoms of these cans are made of steel.

_____ **19.** Tanya or Peg will bring her CD player.

_____ **20.** Will either of the nurses finish their rounds before midnight?

_____ **21.** Some who act in community theaters find his or her future career.

_____ **22.** Nothing that they say give me an idea of what to expect.

_____ **23.** The swarm of hungry locusts are devouring the wheat crop.

_____ **24.** Neither Trent nor Gayla plan to take a vacation at the shore.

_____ **25.** Did you know that three fourths of the food are gone?

Continued ☞

LANGUAGE HANDBOOK **2** **WORKSHEET 9** *(continued)*

EXERCISE D   Most of the following sentences contain errors in subject-verb or pronoun-antecedent agreement. Draw a line through each incorrect verb or pronoun, and write the correct form on the line provided. If a sentence is already correct, write *C*.

EXAMPLES ___*have*___ 1. A few of my classmates ~~has~~ entered the short-story contest.

___*C*___ 2. Manuel doesn't play football, but he watches it on TV.

_____ 1. All of the band's equipment have been unloaded from the bus.

_____ 2. Joseph and Emilio will both have his articles published in the *Hanover High School Star.*

_____ 3. Each of the boys displayed their collage at the front of the classroom.

_____ 4. Gymnastics are one of Teresa's favorite sports to watch during the Olympics.

_____ 5. Here are several akari lamps designed by Isamu Noguchi.

_____ 6. The chess club organize one tournament each spring and one in the fall.

_____ 7. Anybody who completes their test early may spend the rest of the class time in independent reading.

_____ 8. Two thirds of the students were in attendance for the awards ceremony.

_____ 9. Neither Gerald nor Jonathan has read any of Pat Mora's poetry.

_____ 10. Alex don't understand his sister's fascination with bees and other insects.

_____ 11. Today in class either Lucy or Martha will present their oral report on Dr. Helen Rodriguez.

_____ 12. "Those Winter Sundays" is the Robert Hayden poem I've chosen to analyze for my paper.

_____ 13. Have a bouquet of white roses arrived for Mother?

_____ 14. Everyone on the field hockey team practice hard every day.

_____ 15. Both Jeffrey Chapman and Joanna Osburn Bigfeather have works on display at the museum's current art exhibit.

_____ 16. Both of Taro's dogs has been put on the same special diet.

_____ 17. Somebody from the girls' tennis team left their racket lying on the court.

_____ 18. Yolanda and her brother finished his or her chores early so they could go to the concert.

_____ 19. The main attraction of the Tournament of Roses Parade are the colorful floats.

_____ 20. Thirteen dollars are how much I paid for this Kirsty MacColl CD.

Elements of Literature

WORKSHEET 1 | Identifying the Principal Parts of Regular and Irregular Verbs (Rules 3 a–c)

EXERCISE Fill in the blank in each of the following sentences with the correct past or past participle form of the verb given in italics before the sentence.

EXAMPLE *swim* 1. Felipe __*swam*__ well in yesterday's meet.

taste   1. We had never _____ such delicious tomatoes.

suppose   2. We were _____ to read the next chapter.

find   3. Alicia had finally _____ her pen.

go   4. Has Gwen already _____ to the laboratory?

ask   5. The dentist _____ me to return Monday.

sit   6. Last night we _____ out on the patio.

give   7. By noon Sean will have _____ away all of his extra stamps.

lead   8. Benita _____ the children across the street.

sing   9. She has _____ every song in the book.

eat   10. Roger asked if I had _____ the last banana.

begin   11. I had _____ to think you weren't here.

give   12. Have they _____ anything to the rummage sale?

shake   13. Reynard _____ the box of cereal.

swim   14. Has anyone ever _____ across the lake?

be   15. Aunt Ev and Uncle Leo have never _____ there.

drink   16. Aunt Pearl _____ her water in great haste.

bring   17. They had _____ him something to eat.

do   18. Should Denise and I have _____ that job first?

see   19. Yesterday, we _____ the most beautiful sunset!

come   20. At last the lawyer _____ to the point.

set   21. Before I could say anything, he had _____ the plate in front of me.

steal   22. Jean Valjean's troubles with the law began when he _____ a loaf of bread.

drive   23. We had _____ forty miles before we remembered to get gas.

freeze   24. Sometimes the ice on the pond _____ as early as late October.

tear   25. She _____ a page out of her notebook and handed it to me.

| WORKSHEET 2 | Using Irregular Verbs (Rules 3 a–c) |

EXERCISE A   Fill in the blank in each of the following sentences with the correct past or past participle form of the verb given in italics before the sentence.

> EXAMPLE *keep* **1.** The person who has ___*kept*___ our records is not yet here.

ride   **1.** Had Han-Ling _____ a horse before?

drive   **2.** "I have _____ that way before," said Melissa.

throw   **3.** The pitcher had _____ a strike.

steal   **4.** Had they _____ her briefcase?

write   **5.** Before the typewriter was invented, books were _____ by hand.

break   **6.** Was your watch _____ in the scuffle?

fall   **7.** Suzie and Crystal _____ often when they were learning to skate.

swim   **8.** I wish I'd _____ out to the raft after you had.

find   **9.** We had _____ the leftovers.

run   **10.** Stan had just _____ eighty yards for a touchdown.

take   **11.** Althea Gibson must have _____ pride in her tennis skills.

go   **12.** The clerk _____ to the back of the store.

sit   **13.** Yesterday Bret _____ through two movies.

ring   **14.** I didn't know the bell had _____.

bring   **15.** Dad has never _____ his work home with him.

sing   **16.** Silence reigned; not one note was _____.

be   **17.** Helen had never _____ to Japan before.

rise   **18.** Melodie _____ to the occasion and apologized.

tear   **19.** Dale _____ up his poem and started over.

speak   **20.** Miriam Colón _____ to an interviewer about the Puerto Rican Traveling Theatre before the program was televised.

burst   **21.** The pipe had a crack in it before it _____.

fly   **22.** Celia has _____ from Dallas to Miami often.

forget   **23.** Do you think Roscoe has _____ about our meeting?

hide   **24.** We have _____ Dad's birthday present in the attic.

shrink   **25.** Sara's sweater _____ because she put it in a hot dryer.

Continued ☞

EXERCISE B The following paragraphs contain twenty incorrect verbs. Draw a line through each incorrect verb, and write the correct verb form in the space above it. Not every sentence will have an error, but some sentences will have more than one.

                                                                        seen
EXAMPLE [1] I had watched a program about lizards, but I had never ~~saw~~ a Komodo dragon.

[1] Yesterday afternoon our English teacher told us about dragons in literature. [2] I was took aback when she said that dragons actually do exist today. [3] Before the bell rung, she give us our assignment. [4] By Friday we were to turn in compositions we had wrote about the Komodo dragon.

[5] I went to the library immediately after school and begun work on my report. [6] Komodo dragons have exist since prehistoric times. [7] No one knows how these creatures come to the Indonesian island of Komodo long ago. [8] Some scientists think the giant lizards might have swam to the island from Asia, island-hopping along the way. [9] The sight of Komodo dragons in the sea might have gave rise to legends about sea monsters.

[10] These creatures grow up to ten feet long and weigh up to three hundred pounds. [11] Animals unlucky enough to have ran into Komodo dragons have serve as food. [12] One hit with these creatures' massive tails has throwed many an animal several yards. [13] One bite from their powerful jaws has broke many a creature, including humans, in two. [14] Komodos are, however, their own worst enemies. [15] Hungry Komodos, hemmed in by civilization, have took to eating members of their own species. [16] After I had read several articles about these creatures, I was amazed at how much I had learn about them.

[17] That night after dinner, I begun to write my paper. [18] When I ask my brother to read the first page, he was surprise by how little he knew about these lizards. [19] My brother said my paper had bring out the most important facts about the dragons. [20] He had hear of the Komodo dragons, but he did not realize they could grow so large.

LANGUAGE HANDBOOK **3** **USING VERBS**

WORKSHEET 3 | Using the Irregular Verbs *Lie* and *Lay* (Rules 3 a–d)

EXERCISE A   For each of the following sentences, underline the correct form of *lie* or *lay* in parentheses.

> **EXAMPLE 1.** When we came in, we (*lay*, *laid*) our coats on a chair.

1. A heavy mist (*lay*, *laid*) over the valley most of the morning.

2. Before Mother went to work, she (*lay*, *laid*) my bus fare on the table.

3. The Puye Cliff Dwellings (*lie*, *lay*) west of Española, New Mexico.

4. You have (*lain*, *laid*) here on the couch long enough.

5. Someone had (*lain*, *laid*) the cushions on the floor.

6. The sansa, an instrument from Africa, is (*lying*, *laying*) on the display table.

7. His social studies assignment has (*lain*, *laid*) untouched for days.

8. Would the baby rather (*lie*, *lay*) on her back?

9. The old wheelbarrow is (*lying*, *laying*) behind the barn.

10. The movers (*lay*, *laid*) the new rug on the stairs and left for lunch.

EXERCISE B   For each of the following sentences, underline the correct form of *lie* or *lay* in parentheses.

> **EXAMPLE 1.** To prepare for the operation, the doctor (*lay*, *laid*) the bandages and tape out on the table.

1. I couldn't (*lie*, *lay*) down the biography of Harriet Tubman until I'd read the last page.

2. Has the dog been (*lying*, *laying*) in the mud all afternoon?

3. Ella (*lay*, *laid*) her books on the floor.

4. Your tostadas are still (*lying*, *laying*) on the kitchen counter.

5. They had (*lain*, *laid*) a board under each wheel.

6. The ambulance attendants (*lay*, *laid*) him gently on a stretcher.

7. Devon Harbor (*lies*, *lays*) three miles east of here.

8. Your pencil case is (*lying*, *laying*) over there, next to the newspaper.

9. I (*lay*, *laid*) under the car when I was fixing the brakes.

10. Kareem had (*lain*, *laid*) his books on my lunch bag.

Continued ☞

Elements of Literature

NAME _____ CLASS _____ DATE _____

LANGUAGE HANDBOOK **3** **WORKSHEET 3** (continued)

EXERCISE C Write the correct form of *lie* or *lay* in each blank in the following sentences.

EXAMPLES **1.** I told my dog to ___lie___ down. He obeyed and ___lay___ down near the stove. He has been ___lying___ there for an hour.

1. The article on Federico Peña is _____ on my desk. I _____ it there after I finished reading it last night, and it has been _____ there ever since.

2. When I entered, I noticed the tackle box _____ on the floor. Olivia must have _____ the box there yesterday.

3. You will find those clothes _____ in the hamper, where I _____ them last week. They have _____ there for days.

4. A few moments ago I _____ the exhausted cat on the porch. She has been _____ very quietly. With your permission, I will _____ her in a corner of the warm kitchen.

5. I will _____ down on the sofa and read the magazine that is _____ on the table. After I have read it, I will _____ it down where I found it. The magazine will be _____ there when you are ready to read it.

6. Can't some of those books _____ on the shelves until you are ready for them? That way, they won't be _____ in your way.

7. As soon as we came in, we _____ our coats across the chair. By the time we left, the coats had _____ there for two hours.

8. The gardener had been _____ bricks for the new path. He had _____ the bricks in an unusual pattern.

9. In the next few weeks we should _____ out a plan for the vegetable garden that won't require _____ new walkways also.

10. The receptionist _____ the rolled-up posters to one side until she could _____ them out before arranging them on the wall.

Elements of Literature   *Using Verbs* **31**

LANGUAGE HANDBOOK **3** USING VERBS

| WORKSHEET 4 | ### Using the Irregular Verbs *Sit* and *Set* and *Rise* and *Raise* (Rules 3 a–d) |

EXERCISE A For each of the following sentences, underline the correct form of *sit* or *set* in parentheses.

> **EXAMPLES** 1. I was (*sitting*, <u>*setting*</u>) the flowers on the window ledge.
>
> 2. (<u>*Sitting*</u>, *Setting*) in the den, Mother called out that my tutor, Mrs. Martin, was here.

1. "Won't you (*sit*, *set*) here?" I said to Mrs. Martin.

2. She (*sat*, *set*) down and began talking about Newton's laws of motion.

3. "(*Sit*, *Set*) in this chair, Julian," she told me.

4. "Now (*sit*, *set*) that chair out of the way," she went on.

5. I (*sat*, *set*) down as instructed.

6. She showed me how to (*sit*, *set*) an object in motion by propulsion.

7. "As you (*sit*, *set*) here," she said, "lift both feet and kick them out quickly."

8. I did so, and the chair I was (*sitting*, *setting*) in moved backward.

9. (*Sit*, *Set*) the lamp next to the plant, please.

10. Why are you (*sitting*, *setting*) the napkins on top of the plates?

11. Was he (*sitting*, *setting*) by Ms. Agoyo?

12. I thought we had (*sat*, *set*) the box here.

13. Lloyd (*sat*, *set*) down to read "The Jacket," a short story by Gary Soto.

14. Aunt Beth has (*sat*, *set*) in that chair every afternoon this week.

15. I was (*sitting*, *setting*) perfectly still.

16. She asked the pupils to (*sit*, *set*) down their pencils.

17. While we waited for her, we (*sat*, *set*) near the window.

18. Who (*sat*, *set*) these moccasins here?

19. In traditional Japanese homes, people (*sit*, *set*) on cushions.

20. I was (*sitting*, *setting*) up late reading.

21. (*Sitting*, *Setting*) next to her, I enjoyed her conversation.

22. Her house (*sits*, *sets*) by the side of the road.

23. She always (*sits*, *sets*) her pocketbook on the table.

24. The audience (*sat*, *set*) quietly during Ella Fitzgerald's performance.

25. Did you notice where I (*sat*, *set*) my castanets?

Continued ☞

EXERCISE B For each of the following sentences, underline the correct form of *rise* or *raise* in parentheses.

> EXAMPLES 1. The smoke is (*rising*, raising).
>
> 2. The workers will have to (rise, *raise*) the house six inches.

1. The curtain (*rises*, raises), and Celia Cruz takes the stage.

2. The movers (rose, *raised*) the piano with ropes and a pulley.

3. The river has been (*rising*, raising) all night.

4. The crowd had (risen, *raised*) their hero to their shoulders.

5. When the speaker sat down, Mr. Segal (*rose*, raised) to his feet.

6. She was (*rising*, raising) to answer as the bell rang.

7. The model plane (*rose*, raised) a short distance and then dropped.

8. The audience (*rose*, raised) when Maya Angelou approached the podium.

9. The company has (risen, *raised*) her salary.

10. She has (*risen*, raised) as high in her profession as a person can go.

11. Jerry wanted to look at the car's engine, so he (rose, *raised*) the hood.

12. If the water is (raising, *rising*) that quickly, will the dam hold?

13. The general (rose, *raised*) his hand to bid farewell to his troops.

14. The curtain should not (*rise*, raise) until everyone is in place!

15. Our latest project is (*raising*, rising) funds for the new animal shelter.

16. We put so much yeast in the bread dough that it has (rose, *risen*) too fast.

17. Did you notice that the moon (*rose*, raised) earlier each day this week?

18. Amanda had quickly (rose, *raised*) the flags to signal for help.

19. The guide said that the mist always (raises, *rises*) from the swamp.

20. Clouds (*rose*, raised) behind the rainbow, creating a beautiful scene.

21. Stanley finished (rising, *raising*) the clotheslines to the correct height.

22. How does water (*rise*, raise) in the locks of a canal?

23. Julie (*rose*, raised) before anyone else so she could go for a walk.

24. Won't your family be thrilled when you (raise, *rise*) to address Congress!

25. Slowly, the hot-air balloon (*rose*, raised) from its moorings.

LANGUAGE HANDBOOK **3** **USING VERBS**

WORKSHEET 5 | **Using the Right Tense (Rule 3 d)**

EXERCISE On the lines provided, rewrite each of the following sentences by changing the verb(s) to the tense indicated in parentheses.

> **EXAMPLE 1.** Mr. Ignacio helped the Nature Club plan a bird-watching trip. (*present perfect*) _Mr. Ignacio has helped the Nature Club plan a bird-watching trip._

1. Mrs. Wheeler has played tennis or golf every Saturday. (*present*) _____
_____

2. The fans never lost faith in their team's ability to win the close game. (*past perfect*)
_____
_____

3. Chet worked on his biology project for several hours. (*present perfect progressive*)
_____
_____

4. I tried several varieties of *pho,* or Vietnamese noodle soup. (*present perfect*) _____
_____
_____

5. On their vacation, the Duncan family toured the historic buildings of Old San Juan. (*future progressive*) _____
_____

6. By the end of the weekend, Tammy had finished preparing the soil for her flower garden. (*future perfect*)_____
_____

7. Reginald gave a demonstration on how to use a potter's wheel. (*past progressive*)
_____
_____

8. My dog Herbie comes to me as soon as I call him. (*past*) _____
_____

9. Amy played the clarinet solo in the band's final number. (*future*) _____
_____

10. Uncle Brian lived in Taos, New Mexico, for eight years. (*present perfect*)_____
_____

WORKSHEET 6 | **Correcting Needless Changes in Tense (Rule 3 e)**

EXERCISE In the following paragraph, the verb tenses are not consistent. Decide whether the paragraph should be in present or past tense. Then, on the lines provided, rewrite the paragraph, making sure to use consistent verb tense.

EXAMPLE [1] When Keith asked me to go along on his family's camping trip, I tell him to include me.

[1] *When Keith asked me to go along on his family's camping trip, I told him to include me.*

[1] As soon as Mr. and Mrs. Jackson got home from work on Friday, we load the equipment and supplies into the camper. [2] We made it to Bear Creek Lake in just two hours. [3] Not long after we reach the campsite, a mass of gray clouds starts moving in from the west. [4] Mr. Jackson helped Keith and me with our tent, and then we all gather in the camper and eat salads and casseroles. [5] After dinner the fun really starts. [6] The storm hits right after Keith and I settled in the tent for the night. [7] The tent is set up properly and provides excellent protection from the downpour, but it was placed at the foot of a slight incline. [8] As the water washed down the hill, the floor of the tent begins to fill up with water. [9] Keith and I try to tough it out, but after an hour or so we drag our dripping selves to the camper and knocked on the door. [10] Mr. and Mrs. Jackson tried not to laugh as they pull out the extra bed for us.

_____

_____

_____

_____

_____

_____

_____

_____

_____

_____

LANGUAGE HANDBOOK **3** **USING VERBS**

WORKSHEET 7 **Identifying and Using Active and Passive Voice (Rules 3 f, g)**

EXERCISE A Decide whether the verbs in the following sentences are in the active or the passive voice. On the line provided, write *AV* for active voice or *PV* for passive voice.

> EXAMPLE ___*PV*___ **1.** Lacquerware is made by coating an object— such as a wooden box, a plate, or a ceramic vase—with layers of varnish.

_____ **1.** Two sorts of varnish—lacquer and shellac—are used to make lacquer articles.

_____ **2.** Some varnishes create a clear finish, while others have color.

_____ **3.** Each coat of varnish is allowed to dry before another coat is added.

_____ **4.** The varnish forms a shiny, durable, waterproof surface.

_____ **5.** The surface can then be painted, carved, or decorated in some other way.

_____ **6.** The Japanese learned how to create lacquerware from the Chinese, whose lacquer objects date back as far as 300 B.C.

_____ **7.** Beginning in the early 1600s, China and Japan exported lacquerware items, such as chests, cups, and boxes, to Europe.

_____ **8.** European artists soon began to create lacquerware as well, using shellac rather than lacquer.

_____ **9.** Art lovers bought many pieces of European lacquerware in the 1700s.

_____ **10.** The finest examples of the art form, however, were still made in China and Japan.

EXERCISE B Each of the following sentences is written in the passive voice. If the use of the passive voice is appropriate, write *C* on the lines provided. If a sentence is weak or awkward and would be more effective in the active voice, rewrite the sentence by replacing the passive verb with its active form. This revision may involve changing the word order. *Note:* There are four sentences in which the use of the passive voice is acceptable.

> EXAMPLES **1.** The tea kettle was accidentally dropped by Gail. *Gail* *accidentally dropped the tea kettle.*
>
> **2.** Judge Herrera was appointed to the state supreme court in 1998. *C*_____

1. Seeing eye dogs are specially trained to assist visually impaired people. _____

_____

_____

Continued ☞

2. The lawn was mowed and trimmed by Tamisha. _____

_____

_____

3. Many of the tennis matches at this year's French Open were delayed due to rain.

_____

_____

4. The comic strip *Krazy Kat* was drawn by George Herriman from 1913 until 1944.

_____

_____

5. His brand new mountain bike was ridden by Stewart all afternoon. _____

_____

6. Two red, juicy tomatoes and a ripe avocado were carefully selected by Mr. Acosta.

_____

_____

7. News of the interesting new discovery was released to the media early this morning.

_____

_____

8. Their own organic fertilizer, called compost, is made by many gardeners. _____

_____

_____

9. At the Heard Museum, some carved cedar sculptures by John Hoover were seen by my mother.

_____

_____

10. The mysterious package was left on her front doorstep in the middle of the night.

_____

_____

LANGUAGE HANDBOOK **3** **USING VERBS**

WORKSHEET 8 Test (Rules 3 a–g)

EXERCISE A For each of the following sentences, underline the correct verb or verb form in parentheses.

EXAMPLE 1. In 1995 Mia Hamm (*leaded*, *led*) the U.S. women's soccer team to a 19–2–2 record.

1. The Wrights had (*rode*, *ridden*) in the plane twelve seconds.

2. Have you ever (*ate*, *eaten*) bird's-nest soup?

3. They have all (*went*, *gone*) to see the play *Fences*.

4. She often (*sat*, *set*) up all night working.

5. Had he (*wrote*, *written*) two symphonies by 1853?

6. The Oglala Sioux have (*keep*, *kept*) the sun dance as an important part of their culture.

7. We (*saw*, *seen*) many watermelon stands along the road.

8. The architect (*laid*, *lay*) her plans on the table.

9. Flo had (*laid*, *lain*) down to take a quick nap.

10. The fireworks (*began*, *begun*) shortly after dark.

11. I was (*laying*, *lying*) down when you phoned.

12. Please go into the living room and (*sit*, *set*) down.

13. Where have the boys (*went*, *gone*)?

14. She's (*rode*, *ridden*) her bike to school regularly.

15. The bell hasn't (*rang*, *rung*).

16. I just (*lay*, *laid*) a new floor in the kitchen.

17. By four o'clock the sun had (*risen*, *raised*).

18. When the rain started, we (*ran*, *run*) for cover.

19. Aretha Franklin first (*sung*, *sang*) in public at her father's church in Detroit.

20. All day the temperature (*rose*, *raised*) steadily.

21. What happens to the fish after the surface of a lake has (*froze*, *frozen*)?

22. Our science teacher was (*selected*, *select*) as the next principal of this school.

23. The hay has (*grew*, *grown*) especially tall this year.

24. Have you (*spoke*, *spoken*) to your cousin in Mexico lately?

25. Ricky said that he had (*finded*, *found*) a way for the class to meet its goal.

Continued ☞

EXERCISE B   In the following sentences, draw a line through each incorrect verb form and write the correct form on the line provided. If a sentence is already correct, write *C.*

EXAMPLES   *shook*   **1.** Our swarming defense ~~shaken~~ up the other team.

___*C*___   **2.** Len stole the ball and made a layup.

_____ **1.** Have you drank all the lemonade?

_____ **2.** The teacher give me a second chance to improve my score.

_____ **3.** Algebra class has not yet begun.

_____ **4.** Has Mrs. Katakura spoke to you about the tour of Aztec Ruins National Monument?

_____ **5.** Has Lori or Don ever threw curveballs?

_____ **6.** Oh no! My watch was laying on the diving board!

_____ **7.** Have you already eaten all of the tandoori chicken?

_____ **8.** Yesterday, Livvie swum across the lake in record time.

_____ **9.** You could have took the girls with you.

_____ **10.** In his later years, Louis Armstrong played the trumpet less and sung more.

EXERCISE C   The following story contains needless changes in tense. Read through it, and decide whether it should be in present tense or past tense. Then, make the tense consistent by crossing out each incorrect verb and writing the correct form above it.

flared
EXAMPLE [1] Tempers ~~flare~~ as the issue of sports facilities was discussed.

[1] The topic of athletic programs was brought up at the school meeting last Thursday. [2] Neither side listens to the other side. [3] Both were sure the opposing side had a weak case and is merely acting out of ignorance.

[4] Friday, students at Longfellow High School talk about the meeting, and Sylvia Polombo proposes an idea for calming tempers. [5] Longfellow High School has tennis courts available but no swimming pool, and Pershing High School had a swimming pool but no tennis courts. [6] Sylvia suggests that the two schools combine their after-school gym programs so that both groups of students could have the benefit of both facilities.

Continued ☞

[7] The students adopt the proposal and presented it to the principal. [8] Mr. Byrd confers with the principal of Pershing High School. [9] At the next school meeting, he told those present about the students' idea. [10] Influenced by the spirit of cooperation shown by the students, the group settles down and worked out a peaceful solution to the sports issue.

EXERCISE D   On the lines provided, rewrite each of the following sentences by changing the italicized verb or verbs to the tense indicated in parentheses.

EXAMPLE **1.** Ginny *tried* to train the cat to use its scratching post. (*present perfect*) _Ginny has tried to train the cat to use its scratching post._

1. Alicia *is reading* Nina Otero's short-story collection *Old Spain in Our Southwest.* (*present perfect*) _____

_____

2. The storm *damaged* many shops and restaurants in the downtown area. (*past perfect*)

_____

3. The doctor *had completed* her rounds by noon. (*future perfect*) _____

_____

4. Sarah *rehearsed* her part in the play all evening. (*present perfect progressive*) _____

_____

5. Pang *cleaned* the rabbit's cage, and Cynthia *refilled* its water bottle and food dish. (*past progressive*) _____

_____

6. My uncle Len *painted* original designs on furniture and *sold* the pieces at craft fairs. (*present*) _____

_____

7. Megan *will make* bean and cheese burritos for the potluck luncheon. (*past*) _____

_____

8. My friend Yukio *showed* me how to make sushi. (*present progressive*) _____

_____

9. Mr. Payne *taught* both piano and guitar lessons for many years. (*present perfect*) _____

_____

_____

Continued ☞

10. Our class *will visit* the American Museum of Natural History in New York City. (*past*)

_____

_____

EXERCISE E Each of the following sentences is written in the passive voice. If the use of the passive voice is appropriate, write *C* on the lines provided. If a sentence is weak or awkward and would be more effective in the active voice, rewrite the sentence by replacing the passive verb with its active form. This revision may involve changing the word order. *Note:* There are four sentences in which the use of the passive voice is acceptable.

> EXAMPLES **1.** The unsigned letter had been written in green crayon on pale yellow paper. _C_____
>
> **2.** Only two more Margaret Atwood novels are needed by me to make my collection complete. *I need only two more Margaret Atwood novels to make my collection complete.*

1. The new radiator was installed by Aunt Sharon in no time at all. _____

_____

2. The votes were counted and the winners were announced. _____

_____

3. Some of Morgan Freeman's movies have been seen by Peggy and Rhonda. _____

_____

4. Now, the basic steps in custom framing will be demonstrated by Ms. Riley. _____

_____

5. Shirley Chisholm was elected to the U.S. House of Representatives in 1968. _____

_____

6. Finally, the stage was taken by Bonnie Raitt and her band. _____

_____

7. The keys had been accidentally dropped into the trash can by Raymond. _____

_____

8. Graham was rudely awakened by the sound of two cats fighting in the alley. _____

_____

9. Victoria Falls is located in Southern Africa between Zambia and Zimbabwe. _____

_____

10. At his bar mitzvah, parts of the Torah were read in Hebrew by Sidney. _____

_____

LANGUAGE HANDBOOK **4** **USING PRONOUNS**

WORKSHEET 1 | **Using the Nominative Case for Subjects and Predicate Nominatives (Rules 4 a, b)**

EXERCISE A For each of the following sentences, underline the correct pronoun or pair of pronouns in parentheses.

> **EXAMPLE** 1. Mary and (*he*, *him*) often quarrel.

1. Jo and (*she*, *her*) save dimes and pennies.

2. (*We*, *Us*) girls caught a few dogfish.

3. The boys and (*we*, *us*) swam in the deep water.

4. Are (*her and me*, *she and I*) partners?

5. We and (*them*, *they*) met in the finals.

6. Karen and (*I*, *me*) had fruit for dessert.

7. Do you and (*her*, *she*) speak Spanish?

8. You and (*we*, *us*) will work together.

9. Have Arturo and (*them*, *they*) already gone?

10. Stan and (*him*, *he*) look like brothers.

EXERCISE B For each of the following sentences, underline the correct pronoun or pair of pronouns in parentheses.

> **EXAMPLE** 1. The guests of honor are Ted and (*her*, *she*).

1. The first to learn t'ai chi were (*them*, *they*).

2. The most improved tennis player is (*her*, *she*), now that she has mastered the backhand.

3. In this dim light, I thought you were (*he*, *him*).

4. The new president of the company may be (*her*, *she*).

5. The person you saw could not have been (*I*, *me*).

6. The winner will be either Bill or (*him*, *he*).

7. What would you have done if you had been (*they*, *them*)?

8. My best friends are Langston and (*she*, *her*), because they share my interest in soccer.

9. The new pitcher will be either Tony or (*I*, *me*).

10. The ones cooking the gumbo were (*us*, *we*).

WORKSHEET 2	**Using the Objective Case for Direct and Indirect Objects (Rules 4 c, d)**

EXERCISE A   For each of the following sentences, underline the correct pronoun in parentheses.

EXAMPLE 1. Larry surprised Leroi and (*me*, *I*).

1. I will ask my mother and (*she*, *her*) if we can go to the movies.

2. You can believe Jiro and (*I*, *me*).

3. Did anyone tell Estrella and (*she*, *her*) that the time for the concert has changed?

4. I met Sue and (*he*, *him*) at the National Museum of African Art.

5. Will you take (*we*, *us*) to the Cinco de Mayo festival?

6. Do you remember Ella and (*they*, *them*)?

7. I was expecting Harold and (*she*, *her*) to be here by now.

8. You could help (*we*, *us*) tomorrow.

9. I recognized you and (*them*, *they*).

10. Did she mean Nan or (*me*, *I*)?

EXERCISE B   In the following sentences, write an appropriate pronoun in each blank. Use a variety of pronouns, but don't use *you* or *it*.

EXAMPLE 1. Juanita's friends had given ____*her*____ the nickname Xena.

1. Mr. Cohen showed _____ some slides of Yoruban sculptures.

2. Uncle Ned bought Francis and _____ a subscription to *Sports Illustrated*.

3. Marion sent _____ a lovely picture frame as a graduation present.

4. I saw _____ and _____ at the Chinese New Year's Parade.

5. Will you lend _____ this CD?

6. Ms. Choy gave Fred and _____ a chance to solve the math problem.

7. The referee handed _____ the ball at the sideline.

8. Grandpa brought Yori and _____ souvenirs from Venezuela.

9. The architect showed the mayor and _____ the blueprints for the new courthouse.

10. Missy had asked _____ a question about proper rowing techniques.

LANGUAGE HANDBOOK **4** **USING PRONOUNS**

WORSHEET 3 | **Identifying and Using the Objective Case for Objects of Prepositions (Rule 4 e)**

EXERCISE A For each of the following sentences, underline the correct pronoun in parentheses.

EXAMPLE **1.** To Rafael and (*he*, *him*), Richard seems tall.

1. Bill sat behind Nadine and (*I, me*).

2. Will you go to the B. B. King concert with Dad and (*me, I*)?

3. The dog was held pretty tightly between Al and (*her, she*).

4. There were letters for Chen and (*he, him*).

5. No one except you and (*her, she*) saw the play.

6. I played against Alicia and (*they, them*).

7. The work falls to you and (*we, us*).

8. Who was talking to you and (*they, them*)?

9. Come with Gretchen and (*I, me*), and we'll show you how to get to the museum.

10. The story was about Maisie and (*she, her*).

EXERCISE B For each of the following sentences, choose the correct pronoun from the pair in parentheses and write it on the line provided.

EXAMPLE ___*me*___ **1.** Between you and (*I, me*), we were a hit.

_____ 1. The choice is up to Cara and (*she, her*).

_____ 2. My sister borrowed a copy of the book from (*he, him*).

_____ 3. Paul sent presents for Elizabeth and (*her, she*) to their old address.

_____ 4. Would you like to enroll in the class with Nadia and (*me, I*)?

_____ 5. Put the baby in the back seat, between you and (*they, them*).

_____ 6. The invitation to the concert was for Luis and (*we, us*).

_____ 7. Someone besides Miriam and (*them, they*) must have told me about the party.

_____ 8. I sat across from Paulo and (*him, he*) on the train.

_____ 9. Do you want me to give the parcel to you or (*she, her*)?

_____ 10. If you can't come, tell Mr. Ozu instead of Ms. Baxter and (*us, we*).

LANGUAGE HANDBOOK 4 USING PRONOUNS

WORKSHEET 4 | **Identifying and Using Correct Pronoun Forms (Rules 4 a–e)**

EXERCISE A Five uses of nominative and objective pronouns are listed below with their abbreviations. On the first line to the left of each of the following sentences, write the proper abbreviation to indicate how the italicized pronoun is used in the sentence. If the pronoun is incorrect, cross it out and write the correct form on the second line. If the pronoun is already correct, write *C* on the second line.

NOMINATIVE USES
SUBJ = subject of verb
PN = predicate nominative

OBJECTIVE USES
DO = direct object
IO = indirect object
OP = object of preposition

Use | Pronoun
EXAMPLES | _SUBJ_ | _she_ | **1.** Have you or ~~her~~ ever heard of Hob Creek?
| _OP_ | _C_ | **2.** Someone mentioned the creek to *us* girls.

Use | *Pronoun*

_____ | _____ | **1.** It must have been *him* and Kane.

_____ | _____ | **2.** A few of *us* decided to fish there.

_____ | _____ | **3.** Francine and *me* could see the fish.

_____ | _____ | **4.** I quickly called Myra and *she*.

_____ | _____ | **5.** "You and *she* should drop your hooks here!" I yelled.

_____ | _____ | **6.** I and *them* saw two fish approach our hooks.

_____ | _____ | **7.** They really surprised Francine and *I*.

_____ | _____ | **8.** Instead of biting, they gave Myra and *we* a look.

_____ | _____ | **9.** To Francine and *I* they seemed to say, "Fooled you!"

_____ | _____ | **10.** Then they swished their tails and haughtily swam away from *us*.

EXERCISE B For each of the following sentences, underline the correct pronoun in parentheses.

EXAMPLE **1.** Have you and (*them*, *they*) ever been to a Chinese New Year celebration?

1. Did you hear Sally and (*I*, *me*)?

2. We need you and (*her*, *she*) for our softball team.

3. My two lab partners are Don and (*he*, *him*).

4. Aunt Esther offered Ian and (*I*, *me*) some shrimp tempura.

5. The test seemed hard to Lou and (*he*, *him*).

Continued ☞

6. What marks did you and (*her, she*) get in English?

7. Hand Ima or (*he, him*) the soy sauce.

8. Liz and (*she, her*) are going to take Spanish next year.

9. Larry and (*I, me*) would rather take Latin.

10. Every law affects you and (*I, me*).

11. The senator and (*him, he*) have arrived.

12. The camp bus left Mary and (*them, they*) behind.

13. This should be an easy course for you and (*she, her*).

14. Keiko sent (*him, he*) and (*me, I*) letters from Ontario.

15. Did you see Nancy and (*he, him*) at the karate meet?

16. At least, I thought it was (*they, them*).

17. Janet and (*her, she*) were repairing their bicycles.

18. You and (*I, me*) will play against Mom and (*she, her*).

19. The biggest Michelle Kwan fans are (*us, we*).

20. I'll call for you and (*they, them*).

EXERCISE C   Write sentences in which you use the phrases below as indicated by the abbreviations in parentheses.

<table>
<tr><td>NOMINATIVE USES</td><td>OBJECTIVE USES</td></tr>
<tr><td>*SUBJ* = subject of verb</td><td>*DO* = direct object</td></tr>
<tr><td>*PN* = predicate nominative</td><td>*IO* = indirect object</td></tr>
<tr><td></td><td>*OP* = object of preposition</td></tr>
</table>

EXAMPLE 1. Carol and he (*PN*): *That must be Carol and he now.*

1. our parents and us (*DO*): _____

2. our parents and we (*PN*): _____

3. Sasha and they (*SUBJ*): _____

4. Sasha and they (*PN*): _____

5. you and I (*SUBJ*): _____

6. you and me (*IO*): _____

7. you and me (*OP*): _____

8. Kimi or she (*SUBJ*): _____

9. Willis or him (*DO*): _____

10. Willis or him (*OP*): _____

LANGUAGE HANDBOOK 4 USING PRONOUNS

WORKSHEET 5 Special Pronoun Problems (Rules 4 f, g)

EXERCISE A Underline the correct pronoun form in parentheses in each of the following sentences.

> **EXAMPLE 1.** My sister, (*who, whom*) is a gifted artist, wants to study computer animation in college.

1. (*Whoever, Whomever*) wins faces the challenge of lowering this city's crime rate.

2. Tom Flores is a former player (*who, whom*) eventually coached the Seattle Seahawks.

3. Liang wondered (*who, whom*) he should invite to the Halloween party.

4. Alice has not yet found out (*who, whom*) her partner will be.

5. Dorothy is the one to (*who, whom*) I lent my copy of *Annie John.*

6. All the students (*who, whom*) my mom tutors seem to improve fairly quickly.

7. The artist (*who, whom*) she is talking about works mostly in acrylics.

8. I think I know (*who, whom*) the new volleyball champions will be.

9. Mrs. Wallace will help (*whoever, whomever*) wants to try the parallel bars.

10. Black Hawk, (*who, whom*) we are studying in history class, was a Sauk chief.

EXERCISE B Underline the correct pronoun in parentheses in each of the following sentences.

> **EXAMPLE 1.** The two starting guards, Dwayne and (*he, him*), take turns playing point guard.

1. Mr. Tallchief handed the spelling bee winners, Aretha and (*he, him*), their trophies.

2. The team captains, Aleka and (*she, her*), met with the referees before the game began.

3. I found my favorite poets, W. B. Yeats, Maya Angelou, and (*he, him*), on the reading list.

4. The group leaders, Sabina and (*I, me*), assigned each member a specific responsibility.

5. Mr. Newcomb gave (*we, us*) committee members advice about the assembly.

6. My brother plans to go to the Midori concert with two friends—Anthony and (*she, her*).

7. (*We, Us*) wrestlers have an important match coming up next Tuesday.

8. Mrs. Hena asked two groups, (*they, them*) and (*we, us*), for updates on our progress.

9. The speakers at Joe's graduation ceremony were two community leaders—Elena Mercado and (*he, him*).

10. My father, a real estate agent, recently helped find homes for two families, the Morrisons and (*they, them*).

LANGUAGE HANDBOOK **4** USING PRONOUNS

WORKSHEET 6 Using Pronouns with *Than* and *As;* Ensuring Clear Pronoun Reference (Rules 4 h, i)

EXERCISE A   On the lines provided, write the words you would use to complete the incomplete construction. Begin with *than* or *as,* and use the correct pronoun given in parentheses. Some items may have more than one correct answer.

EXAMPLES 1. Sarah likes her more than (*I, me*). *than she likes me*
or *than I do*

2. Is he as popular as (*she, her*)? *as she is*

1. I can't play the conga drums as well as (*she, her*). _____

2. Ms. Weldelkin said Carl did better than (*he, him*). _____

3. These pants fit you better than (*I, me*). _____

4. Mr. Clark praised us more than (*they, them*). _____

5. I can carve turkey better than (*she, her*). _____

6. You are not as forgetful as (*he, him*). _____

7. I expect more of Loretta than (*she, her*). _____

8. They play tennis better than (*we, us*). _____

9. I know you better than (*she, her*). _____

10. He paid Rammel more than (*I, me*). _____

EXERCISE B   Each of the following items contains a pronoun reference that is ambiguous, general, weak, or indefinite. On the lines provided, rewrite each item, correcting the unclear reference.

EXAMPLE 1. Theo is an accomplished saxophone player, and he hopes to make it his career. *Theo is an accomplished saxophone player, and he hopes to make playing the saxophone his career.*

1. The sidewalk was icy in some places. That made our walk to the store very hazardous.

_____

_____

2. Mom asked Debbie to mop the kitchen floor when she got home. _____

_____

_____

Continued ☞

3. They have many Jacob Lawrence paintings in this museum. _____

_____

_____

4. Joan's archaeology class went to the Crow Canyon Archaeology Center in Colorado,
which was very educational. _____

_____

_____

5. Rudy has been working extra hard on his conditioning. That is why Coach Martino is
giving him more playing time. _____

_____

_____

6. I enjoy pottery, especially when I can give them to friends and family as gifts. _____

_____

_____

7. In this issue of the *Northwest High Gazette,* it has a feature article about the Student
Volunteer Association. _____

_____

_____

8. The blizzard continued throughout the night, which made the search team's job even
more difficult. _____

_____

_____

9. My mother told my sister she should swim more often because it is good exercise.

_____

_____

10. Steve is an excellent songwriter, and this one is my favorite. _____

_____

_____

LANGUAGE HANDBOOK **4** USING PRONOUNS

WORKSHEET 7 | Test (Rules 4 a–i)

EXERCISE A   In each of the following sentences, underline the correct pronoun in parentheses. On the line provided, tell how the pronoun is used in the sentence. Write *S* for subject, *PN* for predicate nominative, *DO* for direct object, *IO* for indirect object, or *OP* for object of a preposition.

EXAMPLE _____*S*_____ **1.** Sue and (*her, she*) built a trailer.

_____ **1.** (*They, Them*) and Max saw Chi Wan yesterday.

_____ **2.** It couldn't have been (*her, she*).

_____ **3.** Who was nominated by Leslie and (*him, he*)?

_____ **4.** We gave Julio and (*she, her*) a ride to Syracuse.

_____ **5.** They elected Peg and (*I, me*).

_____ **6.** Are Tama and (*he, him*) ready for their aikido class?

_____ **7.** Did Nina and (*she, her*) get home?

_____ **8.** Mother drove Esther and (*they, them*).

_____ **9.** Were you talking to Alex and (*we, us*)?

_____ **10.** Was that (*she, her*) at Leon's bar mitzvah?

EXERCISE B   In each of the following sentences, draw a line through each incorrect pronoun and write the correct form on the line provided. If a sentence is already correct, write *C*.

EXAMPLES _____*C*_____ **1.** She and her sister volunteered.

_____*I*_____ **2.** Sarah can play tennis better than ~~me~~.

_____ **1.** Have you or he ever seen a flying saucer?

_____ **2.** Tell Richard and I what *reciprocal* means.

_____ **3.** Us boys were in the middle of the lake when the storm hit.

_____ **4.** Can you or they think of a better way to raise money?

_____ **5.** Miss Savalas called Rick and me to her office.

_____ **6.** Has she invited he and Laura?

_____ **7.** The girls have to ride with him and Mrs. Holmes.

_____ **8.** Who packed this lunch for her and Sarah?

_____ **9.** Are you sure it wasn't them and Thelma?

_____ **10.** No, her and Vic were at the movies.

Continued ☞

_____ **11.** That picture didn't appeal to Vera or me.

_____ **12.** Her and Carol will be at camp for two months.

_____ **13.** No, she and Bill went alone.

_____ **14.** She can skate faster than either you or he.

_____ **15.** Who's going sailing with Paula and I?

_____ **16.** He told Toni and I the whole story.

_____ **17.** No one spoke except him and Bob.

_____ **18.** It was the best movie that Yvonne or we had ever seen.

_____ **19.** It was them, all right.

_____ **20.** The play was written by Mr. Godwin and her.

_____ **21.** Mr. Edelman asked for Ned and I.

_____ **22.** My sister looks like my father and I.

_____ **23.** He and Mother went shopping.

_____ **24.** The teacher told Nancy and I about the term paper.

_____ **25.** Karen arrived later than him.

EXERCISE C Underline the correct pronoun in parentheses in each of the following sentences.

> **EXAMPLE 1.** I made Dennis and (*she*, *her*) bookmarks by painting and
> then laminating strips of heavy paper.

1. Anyone (*who*, *whom*) gets a parent's or guardian's permission may go on the field trip.

2. Mr. Ross handed (*we*, *us*) band members copies of the spring practice schedule.

3. Give Margo or (*he*, *him*) that map of the Orlando area.

4. The committee granted Mr. Campos and (*they*, *them*) the funds for their neighborhood improvement project.

5. Mr. Wang, for (*who*, *whom*) my brother works, manages a men's clothing store in the mall.

6. I went to the Indian Art Expo with my cousins, Sonia and (*she*, *her*).

7. The high-scorers for the game were the two starting forwards, Karli and (*she*, *her*).

8. The writer (*who*, *whom*) Gena most admires is Maxine Hong Kingston.

9. Grandmother has sent my brother and (*I*, *me*) train tickets to go visit her in Denver.

10. (*Whoever*, *Whomever*) participates in the walkathon for muscular dystrophy will receive a free T-shirt.

Continued ☞

LANGUAGE HANDBOOK **4** **WORKSHEET 7** *(continued)*

EXERCISE D   Each of the following items contains an unclear pronoun reference. On the lines provided, rewrite each item, correcting the unclear reference.

EXAMPLE **1.** Zack took the turn too fast on his in-line skates. This caused him to fall. *Zack fell when he took the turn too fast on his in-line skates.*

1. Yuki is an exceptionally talented sculptor. She has even sold a few of them. _____

_____

_____

2. The weather was mild, windy, and sunny. This helped make the kite show a success.

_____

_____

3. Mr. Crawford told Dave he had left his tea on the kitchen counter. _____

_____

_____

4. In the movie review it calls Danny Glover's performance "brilliant." _____

_____

_____

5. Our family has been recycling more since the sanitation workers started picking them up at the curb. _____

_____

6. In this magazine they have an article about the Corn Dance Fiesta. _____

_____

7. Kaloma had two poems published in the local literary magazine, which was a dream come true for her. _____

_____

8. When the dog leapt for the stick, it landed in the water. _____

_____

9. Aunt Gretchen sent Jan a letter while she was staying in North Carolina. _____

_____

10. The mail-order company sent the wrong T-shirts. This caused a delay in getting the fund-raiser underway. _____

_____

LANGUAGE HANDBOOK **5** USING MODIFIERS

WORKSHEET 1 | Using Comparative and Superlative Forms of Modifiers (Rules 5 a, b)

EXERCISE A   On the line provided, write the comparative and superlative forms of the modifier given.

EXAMPLES 1. *confidently* <u>more confidently, most confidently, less</u>
<u>confidently, least confidently</u>

2. *fresh* <u>fresher, freshest, less fresh, least fresh</u>

1. *fast* _____

2. *comfortable* _____

3. *fairly* _____

4. *deep* _____

5. *careful* _____

EXERCISE B   On the line provided in each of the following sentences, write the correct form of the modifier shown in italics.

EXAMPLE 1. *well* Josh can swim __<u>better</u>__ now than he could last summer.

1. *good* Lisa is the _____ server on the volleyball team this year.

2. *bad* Mother's cold is _____ today than it was yesterday.

3. *simple* Of the four wallpaper designs, I prefer this one because it is the
_____.

4. *delicious* These are the _____ enchiladas I have ever tasted.

5. *cold* This is the _____ winter we have had in many years.

6. *little* The marching band raised _____ money this year than it did last year.

7. *smooth* This table has a _____ surface than the one in the kitchen.

8. *many* Of all my astronomy books, this one has the _____ illustrations.

9. *well* Mom said that Kristi Yamaguchi skated _____ than the other skaters in the show.

10. *sincere* Both candidates gave impressive speeches, but Ms. Brooks's speech seemed _____.

Continued ☞

EXERCISE C   Most of the following sentences contain errors in the use of comparative and superlative forms of modifiers. Draw a line through each incorrect modifier and write the correct form on the line provided. If a sentence is already correct, write *C*.

EXAMPLES   _funniest_   **1.** Patrick is probably the ~~funnier~~ of all my friends.

_____C_____   **2.** We'll need stronger winds than these to fly my new stunt kite.

_____ **1.** Both of the dishes were spicy, but the stuffed chile peppers were spiciest.

_____ **2.** All of the people on the bus sustained injuries in the crash, but Jerry's were the worse.

_____ **3.** Kyoko speaks Japanese better than her sister does.

_____ **4.** Of all the floats in the parade, this one has more flowers.

_____ **5.** Angel Falls, in eastern Venezuela, is the highest waterfall in the world.

_____ **6.** Barika is the better free-throw shooter on the entire girls' basketball team.

_____ **7.** Which is longest, the Niger River or the Congo River?

_____ **8.** Of all the cities we visited in Italy, Florence was more interesting to me.

_____ **9.** That movie was even worst than the one we saw last weekend.

_____ **10.** Scott Joplin is considered to be the greater of all the ragtime composers.

_____ **11.** We can thank the Germans for the wonderfulest potato salad.

_____ **12.** In creeks near our house, water runs fastest after a thunderstorm than it usually runs.

_____ **13.** The daisies are the less fragile of all the flowers in the bouquet.

_____ **14.** Among American writers, my father thinks Mark Twain is the better.

_____ **15.** Many colors in fabrics can fade, but blue dyes seem to fade more quickly.

_____ **16.** A sour lemon is the less favorite thing I would ever want to eat.

_____ **17.** Of all the cities in Spain, which has the greater population?

_____ **18.** Randall's team ran the mile relay slower than Barry's and Rick's teams.

_____ **19.** The Great Dane is the larger of any dog I have ever seen.

_____ **20.** Of all the countries with a space program, which country's astronauts have logged more hours in space?

LANGUAGE
HANDBOOK **5** USING MODIFIERS

WORKSHEET 2 | **Problems with Using Modifiers (Rules 5 c–e)**

EXERCISE Most of the following sentences contain double comparisons, double negatives, or unclear comparisons. On the lines provided, rewrite each sentence to correct any errors it contains. If a sentence is already correct, write *C.* Some items may have more than one correct answer.

> EXAMPLE 1. Leonard eats more faster than anyone I know. *Leonard eats faster than anyone else I know.*

1. Those are the most loveliest tulips I have ever seen. _____

_____

_____

2. Arlene is a bigger fan of Mariah Carey than anyone in her class. _____

_____

_____

3. Marco misses Miami more than his sister. _____

_____

4. William Gibson is better known than many playwrights. _____

_____

_____

5. Russell is more limber than anyone on his wrestling team. _____

_____

_____

6. Michael Chang is one of the most successfullest tennis players in the world. _____

_____

_____

7. Nina is more reliable than any member of her work group. _____

_____

_____

8. The jewelry inside the store is more expensive than the window. _____

_____

_____

Continued ☞

LANGUAGE HANDBOOK 5 WORSHEET 2 *(continued)*

9. Anthony could hear the leaves rustling, but he couldn't see nothing. _____

_____

_____

10. The island of Honshu has a larger population than that of any other island in Japan. __

_____

_____

11. The paint dried more faster than we thought it would. _____

_____

12. I like the selection of herbs at Tom's Nursery better than Green Garden Square. _____

_____

_____

13. The closets in the new house are not hardly big enough. _____

_____

14. The average temperatures in Portland, Oregon, are lower than those in Phoenix, Arizona. _____

_____

15. Rhode Island is smaller in area than any state in the United States. _____

_____

_____

16. We could not scarcely contain our excitement when we heard the news. _____

_____

_____

17. Maggie writes me more often than Nori. _____

_____

18. Nicholas is taller than anyone in his family. _____

_____

19. Melinda is a more better friend to me than anyone. _____

_____

_____

20. I go swimming with Charles more often than Gordon. _____

_____

_____

Elements of Literature

LANGUAGE HANDBOOK 5 USING MODIFIERS

WORKSHEET 3 **Correcting Dangling Modifiers (Rule 5 f)**

EXERCISE Each of the following sentences contains a dangling modifier. On the lines provided, revise each sentence to eliminate the dangling modifier.

> **EXAMPLE 1.** Even having studied diligently, the social studies test was difficult for me. _Although I had studied diligently, the social studies test was difficult for me._

1. Having been lost in the woods for a couple of hours, the ranger's station was a welcome sight. _____

_____

2. Exploring the fiction section of the city library, several detective novels by Chester Himes were found. _____

_____

3. Before starting to fill the photo album, the photographs should first be arranged in chronological order. _____

_____

4. Falling, the floor was hard when I hit it. _____

_____

5. To preserve your Navajo wool blanket, it must be kept out of direct sunlight. _____

_____

_____

6. Confused by the new material on atoms, many questions were asked. _____

_____

7. To earn money over the summer, my aunt suggested a job at her beauty salon. _____

_____

_____

8. Exhausted after traveling all day, finally walking in the door of our own home was a relief. _____

_____

9. To teach a puppy basic obedience, some study in the use of praise and positive reinforcement is required. _____

_____

10. Stumbling on a loose rock, my footing was lost. _____

_____

LANGUAGE HANDBOOK **5** USING MODIFIERS

WORKSHEET 4 | **Correcting Misplaced Modifiers (Rule 5 g)**

EXERCISE Each of the following sentences contains a misplaced modifier. On the lines provided, revise each sentence, placing the misplaced word, phrase, or clause near the word it modifies.

> **EXAMPLE 1.** Jeremy saw hundreds of beautiful shells strolling along the beach. _Strolling along the beach, Jeremy saw hundreds of beautiful shells._

1. The dog looked as if it needed medical attention that we found on the street. _____

_____

2. The car was towed to the city impoundment lot, which had been parked too close to a fire hydrant. _____

_____

3. Dozens of loud, active monkeys attracted a crowd of spectators inside a spacious cage.

_____

_____

4. The wildlife researcher explained how she tags and tracks wolves in biology class.

_____

_____

5. I think the man ordered the Thai coconut soup in the wool cap. _____

_____

6. The girls viewed a Marisol sculpture touring the Museum of Modern Art. _____

_____

_____

7. Frightened, the store manager helped the little boy find his parents. _____

_____

8. Sean could see an eagle soaring through the powerful binoculars. _____

_____

9. We set the vase on the mantel that Angela had brought. _____

_____

10. The firefighter rescued the boy from the burning building risking her life. _____

_____

_____

LANGUAGE HANDBOOK	**5**	USING MODIFIERS

WORKSHEET 5 | Test (Rules 5 a–g)

EXERCISE A   On the line provided in each of the following sentences, write the correct form of the modifier shown in italics.

> **EXAMPLE 1.** *good*   Lauren is a __*better*__ golfer than she used to be.

1. *many*   Who has _____ kimonos, Mother or Aunt Keiko?

2. *challenging*   This is the _____ game our team has played all season.

3. *gracefully*   Both ballerinas danced well, but Ms. Price seemed to move _____.

4. *much*   Of the three teams in the scavenger hunt, their team covered the _____ ground.

5. *good*   Katherine has a _____ backhand than I do.

6. *short*   Of all the Bernice Zamora poems we have read, this one is the _____.

7. *bad*   The forest fire was bad to begin with, but the rising winds made it even _____.

8. *small*   Of those two puppies, the _____ one seems like the right dog for me.

9. *well*   Mary Jo played _____ than her opponent and won the match.

10. *early*   The bicycle parts that I ordered arrived even _____ than the company had promised.

EXERCISE B   Each of the following sentences contains an error in the use of modifiers. Correct each sentence by crossing out any incorrect words and/or inserting any word or words that are necessary. Use a caret (∧) to show where words will be inserted.

>   *could*
> **EXAMPLES 1.** I ~~couldn't~~ hardly finish the math test before the bell rang.
>
>   *other*
> **2.** Anna likes *Jane Eyre* better than any ∧ book.

1. In my opinion, *The Woman Who Fell from the Sky* was the most entertaining of those two books.

2. Rafael practices harder than anyone in his band.

3. Is Arizona hotter than any state in the country?

4. Karla is the most fastest hurdler on the track team.

Continued ☞

5. Benjamin studies with Latoya more often than with anyone.

6. In my opinion, sunflowers are more prettier than marigolds.

7. Please don't take none of the painting supplies out of this room.

8. The Moo Shu duck that my dad makes is better than the Chinese restaurant downtown.

9. I visit Aunt Patricia more often than Aunt Luisa.

10. That bookstore doesn't have no magazines on architecture or landscape design.

EXERCISE C   Most of the following sentences contain dangling or misplaced modifiers. On the lines provided, revise each sentence so that it makes sense. If a sentence is already correct, write *C.*

> **EXAMPLE 1.** Browsing through the gift shop, many unique lamps were displayed. _Browsing through the gift shop, we saw many_ _unique lamps on display._

1. We found a box of slides taken by my grandfather in the trunk under the stairs. _____

_____

_____

2. When she was in elementary school, my mother showed me some stories she had written. _____

_____

3. Having neglected to drink enough water, dehydration set in during the tennis player's match. _____

_____

4. The man put the baby into the crib that had fallen asleep. _____

_____

5. Surrounded by adoring fans, autographs were signed for twenty minutes. _____

_____

_____

6. To prepare the terrarium, first a layer of small pebbles should be placed on the bottom for drainage. _____

_____

Continued ☞

7. The woman will be giving a talk about Aztec mythology in the green suit. _____
_____
_____

8. To become a good photographer, both technical skill and an artistic sense are needed.
_____
_____

9. While living in Puerto Rico, Mr. Hoffman learned to speak Spanish well. _____
_____
_____

10. Diego rode over a rugged trail on his mountain bike that was two miles long. _____
_____
_____

11. Cracked and dusty from the drought, the farmer surveyed his soil. _____
_____
_____

12. While walking on the beach, the smell of the sea air was refreshing. _____
_____
_____

13. Staying in Memphis several days, the National Civil Rights Museum was visited. _____
_____
_____

14. Scurrying up a nearby tree, the squirrel escaped from the pursuing dog. _____
_____
_____

15. Juanita read about the building that had been demolished in the Sunday paper. _____
_____
_____

16. Dangling from a strand of web, Dana spotted a spider. _____
_____
_____

Continued ☞

17. Thrilled by the tournament win, a special celebration was planned. _____

_____

_____

18. Gazing at the colorful, peaceful aquarium, Craig began to relax. _____

_____

_____

19. I found this book on the bottom shelf, which was written by Elie Wiesel. _____

_____

_____

20. While vacuuming the carpet, the cat ran to the bedroom and hid under the bed. _____

_____

_____

21. By walking slowly over the rocky terrain, fossils were easy to find. _____

_____

_____

22. Hungry, the sandwiches soon disappeared from the children's plates. _____

_____

_____

23. Losing their shingles in the strong wind, the hurricane lashed the beachfront cottages.

_____

_____

24. After successfully completing the secret experiment, the scientist gave the solution to his assistant for safekeeping. _____

_____

_____

25. Flying north in a V-formation, the farmer noticed a large flock of geese. _____

_____

_____

WORKSHEET 1 | Identifying Phrases and Prepositional Phrases
(Rules 6 a, b)

EXERCISE A Identify which of the following word groups are phrases and which are not. On the line provided, write *PHR* if the word group is a phrase and *NP* if it is not a phrase.

EXAMPLE ___PHR___ **1.** throughout the night

_____ **1.** the fried rice   _____ **4.** Sarah is pushing my bobsled

_____ **2.** with a shovel   _____ **5.** Nori and her

_____ **3.** in front of them

EXERCISE B For each of the following items, complete the prepositional phrase by writing an appropriate object on the line provided.

EXAMPLE **1.** before the _concert_

1. beyond the _____   **4.** in addition to _____

2. except _____ and _____   **5.** to _____ and _____

3. during a _____

EXERCISE C Draw a line under each prepositional phrase in the following paragraph. Then, circle the object of each preposition. There are twenty-five prepositional phrases.

EXAMPLE [1] <u>In the early</u> (morning) New Yorkers crowd the fish market.

[1] Along the wharves beside the East River in the shadow of the Brooklyn Bridge stands the Fulton Fish Market, perhaps the world's busiest market. [2] During the hours before dawn, the market springs into action as people unload their boats and lay their wares at the feet of the tall skyscrapers. [3] Buyers and sellers conduct their business in a rising crescendo of noise, which by early morning exceeds the noises coming from the heart of the city. [4] Inside, the market is jammed to the ceiling with crated fish from distant places, iced and ready to be distributed throughout the city. [5] The market is no place for the squeamish. [6] The smell is what you would expect; the sounds are deafening. [7] On the boats there are many "colorful characters," dressed for the weather, their faces made leathery by Atlantic winds. [8] Before noon the last fish has been sent on its way, and the last deck has been hosed down. [9] Fish for dinner, anyone?

| WORSHEET 2 | Using and Identifying Adjective Phrases (Rule 6 b) |

EXERCISE A   On the line provided, add an adjective phrase to each of the following nouns and pronouns. Do not use the same preposition twice.

EXAMPLE **1.** a man _on a horse_ _____

1. the highway _____

2. the one _____

3. a window _____

4. letters _____

5. a book _____

6. everyone _____

7. the girl _____

8. a necklace _____

9. a school _____

10. houses _____

EXERCISE B   Replace each adjective phrase in the following sentences with a single adjective that has the same meaning as the phrase. Underline the adjective phrase. On the first line at the left, write the adjective that replaces the phrase. On the second line, write the noun the adjective modifies.

Adjective   _Word modified_
Western   _tales_   EXAMPLE **1.** Tales <u>about the West</u> are popular.

_____   _____   **1.** I like stories with ghosts.

_____   _____   **2.** Winds in March often disturb me.

_____   _____   **3.** Finally, I bought a chest for tools.

_____   _____   **4.** Fins on fish can injure anglers.

_____   _____   **5.** He needed words of encouragement.

_____   _____   **6.** The gentleman from France nodded.

_____   _____   **7.** I used a hammer with a claw.

_____   _____   **8.** A boat for racing had sunk.

_____   _____   **9.** Basketball is a game of action.

_____   _____   **10.** Storms during the spring are sudden.

Continued ☞

EXERCISE C   In the following paragraph, underline each adjective phrase. Then, draw an arrow to the word it modifies. There are twenty adjective phrases to identify.

EXAMPLES   [1] The students in Mrs. Liu's class pondered the container.

[2] The jar of water on the desk nearly spilled.

[1] Water normally takes the exact shape of its container. [2] When water reaches a level beyond a jar's capacity, the water at the top spills out. [3] This behavior of liquids is one of the principal reasons for clogged gas burners on kitchen stoves. [4] A trick from a newspaper column certainly baffled the students in my science class. [5] The water-filled glass on Mrs. Liu's desk contained a number of pennies. [6] The water above the rim was not spilling! [7] A classmate behind me exclaimed, "Wow! The water in that glass must be supernatural!" [8] Conversation between the teacher and me soon gave everyone the right key to the mystery concerning the water level. [9] The pennies in the glass had been immersed carefully, thus slowly raising the level of the water. [10] The surface tension of the water prevented its spilling.

EXERCISE D   Write a sentence using each italicized adjective phrase below. Underline the word that the phrase modifies.

EXAMPLE   **1.** *at that store*   The authors at that store were busily autographing their books.

1. *for the party* _____

_____

2. *to the new park* _____

_____

3. *of the latest survey* _____

_____

4. *in that long line* _____

_____

5. *of my friends* _____

_____

LANGUAGE HANDBOOK **6** PHRASES

WORKSHEET 3 | **Identifying Adverb Phrases and Adjective Phrases (Rule 6 b)**

EXERCISE A   Each of the following sentences contains an adverb phrase. Underline each adverb phrase, and draw an arrow from the phrase to the word or words it modifies. On the line provided, write what the phrase tells: *how, when, where, why,* or *to what extent.*

EXAMPLE ___how___ **1.** The truth about ancient civilizations often is revealed <u>through archaeological studies</u>.

_____ **1.** For many years people have sought the lost continent Atlantis.

_____ **2.** Some people claim it was situated off the Spanish coast.

_____ **3.** Others believe that fabled Atlantis actually existed in the Aegean Sea.

_____ **4.** They argue with certainty that a Greek island named Thera was Atlantis.

_____ **5.** Between 1620 and 1500 B.C., Thera experienced a violent volcanic eruption.

_____ **6.** Because of this eruption, a city on the island was buried.

_____ **7.** Tidal waves and earthquakes occurred after the eruption.

_____ **8.** The island's flourishing civilization was lost in the disaster.

_____ **9.** Archaeologists who worked on Thera unearthed the buried city.

_____ **10.** Many scholars were excited because of this research.

EXERCISE B   Underline each adverb phrase in the following sentences. Then, draw an arrow from the adverb phrase to the word or words it modifies.

EXAMPLE **1.** Some *Star Trek* fans watch *Star Trek: Voyager* <u>at every opportunity</u>.

1. Luis and I have watched episodes of *Star Trek: Voyager* for several years.

2. We have viewed each show with avid interest.

3. I even know the dialogue for some of the shows by heart.

4. A devoted group of *Star Trek* fans has developed over the years.

5. One year they held a *Star Trek* convention in New York City.

6. Luis and I attended the convention out of curiosity.

7. A small replica of *Voyager* stood near the center of the room.

8. We were curious about the replica.

9. A miniature of Kathryn Janeway sat in the captain's chair.

10. Testing the circuitry, Harry Kim lay beneath the operations console.

Continued ☞

EXERCISE C Underline the prepositional phrase in each sentence, and draw an arrow from the phrase to the word it modifies. On the line provided, identify how the phrase is used. Write *ADJ* for adjective or *ADV* for adverb.

EXAMPLE ___ADV___ **1.** The coach was pacing along the sideline.

_____ **1.** The tamales at this restaurant are delicious.

_____ **2.** Pam writes with her left hand.

_____ **3.** From the north came a driving snowstorm.

_____ **4.** The sculpture by Augusta Savage is inspiring.

_____ **5.** The book was based on an actual event.

_____ **6.** Teams from twenty schools entered the tournament.

_____ **7.** Buy your school supplies at Zing's.

_____ **8.** We won a vacation in Florida.

_____ **9.** Marie Curie's achievements in science were remarkable.

_____ **10.** Kristi Yamaguchi won a gold medal at the 1992 Olympics.

EXERCISE D Underline each prepositional phrase in the following paragraph. In the space above each prepositional phrase, tell what kind of phrase it is by writing *ADJ* for adjective phrase or *ADV* for adverb phrase. A sentence may have more than one prepositional phrase, or a sentence may have no prepositional phrases.

　　　　　　　　　　ADJ　　　　　ADJ　　　　　　ADJ　　　　　　　　ADV
EXAMPLE [1] Millions of people in the deserts of Africa and Asia depend on camels.

[1] Beyond a doubt, the camel is one of the strangest domesticated animals. [2] The camel does not always express affection for human beings. [3] A camel with a grievance will often spit at, bite, or kick its owner or anyone in its vicinity. [4] This has not created goodwill between humans and camels. [5] If people suddenly disappeared from the earth, the camel could survive on plants and grasses that most other animals would ignore. [6] It has never become dependent upon humans. [7] The average camel can carry almost four hundred pounds on its back without showing signs of tiring. [8] Each camel has its own limit. [9] If the owner goes beyond the limit by even a minute amount, the camel will suddenly collapse under the load from the strain and perhaps die. [10] This fact is the basis for the saying, "That was the straw that broke the camel's back."

LANGUAGE HANDBOOK **6** PHRASES

WORKSHEET 4 | **Identifying Participles and Participial Phrases (Rule 6 c)**

EXERCISE A Underline the participles used as adjectives in each of the following sentences.

> **EXAMPLE 1.** The <u>laughing</u> children climbed onto the merry-go-round.

1. Early in the morning, three chattering blue jays woke me up.

2. The Cinco de Mayo party on our block is always the best-attended event of the year.

3. The unclaimed luggage at the airport was taken to the security office.

4. Young turkeys are called poults, and grown turkeys are called hens or toms.

5. Ascending the rock face, my sister waved to us.

6. The shivering sheep huddled together out of the wind.

7. The Great Wall of China was begun in the third century B.C. as a protecting barrier.

8. Our family is going to an amusement park to ride its towering roller coasters.

9. The house next door is completely decorated with found objects.

10. When the attacking wasps swarmed around him, Jon stood still and was not stung.

EXERCISE B Underline each participial phrase in the following sentences.

> **EXAMPLE 1.** The deer, <u>swimming rapidly</u>, reached the riverbank safely.

1. Sojourner Truth, determined to express her ideas, influenced many people in Akron in 1852.

2. Hoping to solve the puzzle, Michel researched several subjects.

3. Senator Juarez, campaigning for re-election, spoke downtown last week.

4. The saris, imported from India, are made of beautiful, colorful silk.

5. Sleeping on the desert floor, Jimmy woke to find a rattlesnake coiled on his chest.

6. The robin's nest, shaken by the strong wind, fell from the tree branch to the ground.

7. Laughing and shouting loudly, our soccer team, now district champions, left the field.

8. The snow falling through the light from the street lamp is beautiful to watch.

9. Riding one horse and leading three others, Martha returned to the ranch.

10. Ghana, situated on the Gulf of Guinea, is one of several countries in West Africa.

LANGUAGE HANDBOOK **6** **PHRASES**

| **WORKSHEET 5** | **Identifying Gerunds and Gerund Phrases (Rule 6 d)** |

EXERCISE Underline each gerund or gerund phrase in the following sentences. Then, above each underlined word or phrase, identify its use as *S* (subject), *PN* (predicate nominative), *DO* (direct object), or *OP* (object of a preposition).

S

EXAMPLE 1. Swimming is my favorite sport.

1. Camping was fun until the mosquitoes found us.

2. In addition to biking, Dave runs and lifts weights each day.

3. I wonder why the CD player stopped working.

4. For Black History Month, class assignments include studying Romare Bearden's paintings.

5. By adopting techniques of cubist painters, Bearden colorfully recorded scenes of African American life.

6. Bearden's skill at painting is evident in his silk-screen work *Jazz*.

7. Bearden showed great style and flair by using different media.

8. The cats outsmarted the dog by climbing the tree.

9. Writing is a pleasure for some people and a chore for others.

10. The Spanish Club enjoyed serving empanadas at the Multicultural Fair.

11. Watering the plants was the last thing we did before we left the house.

12. One of Tasha's talents is writing poetry.

13. The aviation historian enjoys discussing zeppelins.

14. Some really strange colors resulted from combining the paint pigments.

15. Linking two railroad cars together can be difficult.

16. On the swim team, Carlos's specialty is diving from the high board.

17. I wanted to write my own life stories after reading Sandra Cisneros's fiction.

18. Constructing the skyscraper took ten years.

19. The best part of the Buffalo River trip was white-water canoeing.

20. In-line skating is a popular sport.

21. Try whistling this.

22. Directing films is hard work, but often fun.

23. One of the jobs of a film director is giving instructions to the actors.

24. Jennifer broke our school record by running the mile faster than anyone else in our class.

25. Trying new foods broadened Jim's horizons.

WORKSHEET 6 Identifying Infinitives, Infinitive Phrases, and
Infinitive Clauses (Rules 6 e, f)

EXERCISE Underline the infinitives, infinitive phrases, and infinitive clauses in the
following sentences. Then, identify each infinitive or infinitive phrase as *N* (noun),
ADJ (adjective), or *ADV* (adverb), and each infinitive clause as *CL* (clause). A sentence may
contain more than one infinitive, infinitive phrase, or infinitive clause.

                                                    ADJ
          EXAMPLE **1.** This is the route <u>to take</u>.

1. When did he learn to broad jump?

2. We joined our guide and asked him to identify the formations in the cave.

3. To err is human; to forgive is divine.

4. In Shakespeare's time, acting companies needed to have wealthy patrons.

5. The Keller family hired Anne Sullivan to teach their daughter Helen.

6. Harriet A. Jacobs, a runaway slave, struggled in dim light to read and to sew.

7. To give life to the common things of childhood is one aim of Gary Soto's writing.

8. Zitkala-Sa, a Yankton Sioux, went east to attend school.

9. Richard Wright wanted to escape from the poverty of his childhood.

10. My goal is to read Wright's *Black Boy*.

11. To learn is our main purpose at school.

12. If you are going to Albany, the bus to board is number twenty-seven.

13. For many people, a challenging mountain to climb is Denali.

14. Kim is always happy to help.

15. The ingredients you need to make the stir-fry are in the refrigerator.

16. To argue is her whole reason for talking.

17. To learn darkroom techniques is easy if you take photography classes.

18. Annie likes exploring and encourages me to follow her.

19. Diane's dog Doofus would go fetch anything.

20. This is the final quotation to identify.

21. To treat others fairly should be a goal for everyone.

22. Tamara decided to drive to Philadelphia rather than to fly.

23. Her brother Charlie was happy to have her visit him.

24. My mom asked me to pick her up at the train station.

25. Her plan to take the plane didn't fit her schedule.

LANGUAGE HANDBOOK 6 PHRASES

| WORSHEET 7 | **Identifying and Using Appositives and Appositive Phrases (Rule 6 g)** |

EXERCISE A Underline the appositive or appositive phrase in each of the following sentences. Underline twice the word or words that each appositive identifies or explains.

> EXAMPLE 1. Bailey, my sister's cat, weighs twelve pounds.

1. Komodo dragons, giant flesh-eating monitor lizards, grow to be over eleven feet long.

2. These huge reptiles, the largest lizards in the world, live in some Southeast Asian jungles.

3. They are named after Komodo Island, a part of Indonesia.

4. Other monitor lizards, the perenty and the water monitor, live in tropical areas of Australia and Southeast Asia.

5. The unusual name *monitor* is applied to these lizards because people believe that they warn of the presence of crocodiles.

6. My sister Sarah wants to be a writer.

7. One of the most famous playwrights in history, William Shakespeare wrote tragedies, comedies, and romances.

8. In a film version of one Shakespeare play, Kenneth Branagh plays Hamlet, the prince of Denmark.

9. Branagh also directed the film *Henry V*.

10. In that film, he plays the title character, King Henry V of England.

EXERCISE B Create an original appositive or an appositive phrase to explain or identify at least one of the nouns or pronouns in each of the following sentences.

> EXAMPLE 1. Scrambler just chewed up our garden hose. *Scrambler, our pet Rottweiler, just chewed up our garden hose.*

1. Gabriel Gomez has retired. _____
_____

2. Forty-seven people have accepted the invitation to the Kwanzaa party. _____
_____

3. Our speaker will be Lee Anna Wilkes. _____
_____

4. Next year Hector Ortiz will run in the marathon. _____
_____

5. Carla's favorite writer is Alice Walker. _____
_____

WORKSHEET 8 Test (Rules 6 a–g)

EXERCISE A On the line provided, for each of the following sentences, write a participle or participial phrase that completes the meaning of the sentence.

EXAMPLE **1.** The _setting_ sun turned the clouds purple.

1. The coach, _____ before the game, encouraged us to do our best.

2. The _____ children were eagerly hitting the piñata.

3. The bear, _____, peered at us through the fence.

4. _____, the horses came toward the barn.

5. The _____ fortress is visible for miles.

6. A _____, mountainous road leads to the castle.

7. _____, Igor shuffles to the door.

8. The door, _____, opens slowly.

9. _____ rain fell through the leaves of the trees.

10. _____, I enter the front hall.

EXERCISE B Underline each gerund or gerund phrase in each of the following sentences. On the line provided, identify the gerund or gerund phrase as *S* (subject), *PN* (predicate nominative), *DO* (direct object), or *OP* (object of a preposition).

EXAMPLE _____S_____ **1.** Traveling is my favorite summer pastime.

_____ **1.** Why do people enjoy flying?

_____ **2.** Getting to other countries is fast and easy by plane.

_____ **3.** By reading, you can learn about a place before you visit it.

_____ **4.** One way to travel is touring with a group.

_____ **5.** Visiting Rome appeals to some people interested in history.

_____ **6.** Many travelers enjoy climbing the numerous ancient steps in Rome.

_____ **7.** Throwing coins in the Trevi Fountain guarantees one's return to this thrilling city, or so the legend says.

_____ **8.** One of the great pleasures in Rome is partaking of the wonderful pastas, vegetables, and fruits.

_____ **9.** Going only a short distance from Rome lets you see the ruins of the city's ancient seaport, Ostia Antica.

_____ **10.** You will be amazed at structures capable of standing for centuries.

Continued ☞

EXERCISE C   Underline the infinitives, infinitive phrases, and infinitive clauses in the following sentences. On the line provided, identify each infinitive or infinitive phrase as *N* (noun), *ADJ* (adjective), or *ADV* (adverb), and each infinitive clause as *CL* (clause).

EXAMPLE _____N_____ **1.** He hoped <u>to go to college</u>.

_____ **1.** Coach Chen agreed to lead the sports rally.

_____ **2.** The apples to sell are the ones in the baskets.

_____ **3.** To attend is not always enough.

_____ **4.** The dog pulled Jody by the arm and helped to free him from the wreck.

_____ **5.** Our trip to see my Apache grandmother in Arizona was fun.

_____ **6.** To replace the valves in a car engine takes more than a day.

_____ **7.** Are you going to Mexico to study Diego Rivera's art?

_____ **8.** To be called soluble, a substance must be one that can be dissolved in a liquid.

_____ **9.** Alicia's aunt speaks Greek, and Alicia wants her to teach us a few phrases.

_____ **10.** The volcanoes to avoid are the active ones.

EXERCISE D   Underline the appositive(s) or appositive phrase(s) in each of the following sentences. Then, underline twice the word or words that each appositive identifies or explains.

EXAMPLE **1.** <u>Neon</u>, <u>an inert gas</u>, is used in some lighted signs.

1. Actor and songwriter George M. Cohan wrote many songs that are still sung today.

2. *Trompe l'oeil,* "trick of the eye," is a fascinating type of art to examine.

3. The Spanish explorer Cabeza de Vaca was shipwrecked near present-day Galveston, Texas, in 1528.

4. Neptune, the Roman god of the sea, is identified with the Greek god Poseidon.

5. A dissident, someone in disagreement with official policy, may be jailed for speaking out in some countries.

6. My brother Mike is looking for a good book to read.

7. Many grazing animals in the Arctic eat reindeer moss, a gray lichen.

8. My niece Nicoletta enjoys reading.

9. Our dog Arf is a mongrel of unknown parentage.

10. Risotto, rice cooked with broth, is a popular food in Italy.

LANGUAGE HANDBOOK **7** CLAUSES

WORKSHEET 1 | **Identifying Independent and Subordinate Clauses (Rules 7 a–c)**

EXERCISE A   In the following paragraphs, underline each independent clause once, and underline each subordinate clause twice.

> **EXAMPLE** [1] <u>One group created a multimedia presentation</u> <u><u>that described the ecology of a tropical rain forest</u></u>.

[1] After our class had studied various ecological systems, Mrs. Roth suggested that we divide into groups and choose an interesting project. [2] The project that we chose was building a woodland terrarium. [3] After school was over, we went to a wooded park where we hunted for materials. [4] Leilani found several flowering plants such as wintergreen, whose flowers are white and bell-shaped, and pipsissewa, which has leaves that once were used for medicinal purposes. [5] She put the plants in cut-off milk containers whose bottoms were filled with soil. [6] While I was looking for a mossy rock, I found a salamander. [7] Although it was quite fast, I managed to get a good look at it.

[8] The next day, Mrs. Roth said that we could use the aquarium tank from the science closet. [9] First, we covered the base of the tank with gravel so that the soil would have adequate drainage, and then we added a layer of woodland soil. [10] After we planted small ferns and seedlings, we placed the terrarium in a cool spot.

EXERCISE B   The subordinate clauses in the following sentences are italicized. Underline the subject of each subordinate clause once and the verb twice.

> **EXAMPLE 1.** *As the <u>curtain</u> <u><u>rose</u></u>*, Clay, *<u>who</u> <u><u>had</u></u> the leading role*, was feeling nervous.

1. *If failures do not quit,* they may eventually succeed, *as U. S. Grant did.*

2. *When Janice was ill,* she read Katherine Mansfield's "Miss Brill," *which you had recommended.*

3. *After I had overcome my stage fright,* I remembered *what my next line was!*

4. Mr. Habeeb, *who is a superb teacher,* answers questions *that the class should have asked.*

5. *When class discussion ended,* Ms. Jones read "Ain't I a Woman?" *which is a speech by Sojourner Truth.*

LANGUAGE
HANDBOOK **7** **CLAUSES**

WORSHEET 2 | **Identifying and Using Adjective Clauses (Rule 7 d)**

EXERCISE A   Underline each of the adjective clauses in the following sentences. Draw an arrow from the clause or clauses to the word or words it modifies.

EXAMPLE 1. The pony express, <u>which was the first postal system in the West</u>, carried mail from Missouri to California.

1. Do you know any people who have emigrated from the United States to Israel?

2. Ynes Mexia was an explorer whose main interest was botany.

3. Last summer Mona visited Spokane, which is her birthplace.

4. Satire, which is a kind of writing, makes fun of people or actions that are absurd.

5. Opossums that are cornered have a unique method of self-defense.

6. Toni Morrison wrote a book that won the Pulitzer Prize.

7. A person whom others call "lucky" is usually an intelligent hard worker who takes full advantage of opportunities.

8. The dog that was gnawing a large soup bone growled at me.

9. Ralph J. Bunche, who won the Nobel Peace Prize in 1950, was a U.S. diplomat.

10. Roberto Clemente was a leader on the Pittsburgh Pirates team that won the 1971 World Series.

EXERCISE B   Combine each of the following pairs of sentences by changing one sentence into an adjective clause. Write your revisions on the lines provided.

EXAMPLE 1. John Martin speaks Spanish fluently. He lived in Mexico for two years. *John Martin, who lived in Mexico for two years,* *speaks Spanish fluently.*

1. My friend helped me with my serve. She is an excellent tennis player. _____

_____

_____

2. Jane Smiley will be at the bookstore. She will be autographing copies of her new book there. _____

_____

_____

Continued ☞

3. The gold nugget was about the size of a pea. The nugget set off the California gold rush. _____

_____

_____

4. That organization works to protect whales. They are threatened with extinction. ____

_____

_____

5. Cassava is an important food in Africa. It is usually mashed into a gelatin called *fufu* to accompany stews and soups. _____

_____

_____

6. The firefighters will be honored by a parade. They rescued six children from a burning building. _____

_____

_____

7. Dogs and cats see only in black and white. They are colorblind. _____

_____

_____

8. Martina Arroyo sings opera around the world. She grew up in New York City. _____

_____

_____

9. N. Scott Momaday has written several novels. They draw upon his Kiowa and Cherokee heritage. _____

_____

_____

10. The journalist just received the Pulitzer Prize. I talked to that journalist. _____

_____

_____

WORKSHEET 3 | Identifying Adverb Clauses and Adjective Clauses (Rules 7 d, e)

EXERCISE A In each of the following sentences, underline the adverb clause and circle the subordinating conjunction. On the line provided, write the letter of the item that shows what the clause tells about the word it modifies.

> **a.** how **c.** where **e.** to what extent
>
> **b.** when **d.** why **f.** under what conditions

EXAMPLE ___*b*___ **1.** (When) you are near a hot stove, notice the rising air.

_____ **1.** Hot air is much lighter than cold air is.

_____ **2.** When the warm air rises, the cool air rushes underneath.

_____ **3.** Because this movement occurs, sea breezes blow inland.

_____ **4.** Is there no wind unless the temperature of air varies?

_____ **5.** Before you answer, you must know about prevailing winds.

_____ **6.** Wherever the climate is hot, air rises rapidly.

_____ **7.** Air goes downward wherever the climate is cold.

_____ **8.** Tropical air travels toward the poles as the polar air moves toward the equator.

_____ **9.** We must not act as if this is the complete picture.

_____ **10.** As the earth rotates, the rotation affects wind direction.

EXERCISE B Underline the subordinate clause in each of the following sentences. Then, on the line provided, write *ADJ* if it is an adjective clause or *ADV* if it is an adverb clause.

EXAMPLE ___*ADJ*___ **1.** There's a car that looks just like ours.

_____ **1.** *Dom Casmurro* is the novel that most critics regard as Joaquim Maria Machado de Assis's masterpiece.

_____ **2.** The calendar that we use today was introduced in 1582.

_____ **3.** It was Alec and Clara who put life into that party!

_____ **4.** I shall write when I receive your new address.

_____ **5.** If I hear any news, I will call you.

_____ **6.** Although taxes are unpopular, they are necessary.

_____ **7.** Take the road that follows the coast.

_____ **8.** Don't volunteer unless you want to work.

_____ **9.** I saved all the money you gave me.

_____ **10.** Gabriela Mistral wrote poetry while she worked as a teacher and principal.

LANGUAGE HANDBOOK	**7**	CLAUSES

WORKSHEET 4
Identifying Noun Clauses and Subordinate Clauses
(Rules 7 c–f)

EXERCISE A   Underline the noun clause in each of the following sentences. On the line provided, tell how the clause is used. Use the abbreviation *S* for subject, *PN* for predicate nominative, *DO* for direct object, or *OP* for object of a preposition.

EXAMPLE ___DO___ **1.** Do you know <u>why a photographer uses a flash</u>?

_____ **1.** I know that plantains are used in African cooking.

_____ **2.** That he was safe on second seemed obvious to me.

_____ **3.** Michelle Kwan must know how important good skates are.

_____ **4.** I'll take whoever wants a ride.

_____ **5.** This is what she gave me.

_____ **6.** Whoever gets the job will have to work hard.

_____ **7.** A new athletic field is what we need most.

_____ **8.** I wrote about what I did last summer.

_____ **9.** Where Marian went remained a secret.

_____ **10.** We read that large sculptures often decorated ancient Aztec structures.

EXERCISE B   Underline the subordinate clause in each of the following sentences. On the line provided, tell how the clause is used. Use the abbreviation *ADJ* for adjective clause, *ADV* for adverb clause, or *N* for noun clause.

EXAMPLES ___ADJ___ **1.** Superstitions <u>that people believe</u> can be amazing.

___N___ **2.** Do you think <u>that superstitions are true</u>?

_____ **1.** If a mirror breaks, seven years of bad luck supposedly follow.

_____ **2.** A mirror that is broken should be buried.

_____ **3.** As some people think, spilled salt means bad luck.

_____ **4.** Toss a pinch of salt over your left shoulder whenever you accidentally spill some.

_____ **5.** That is what will protect you from bad luck.

_____ **6.** If you walk under a ladder, make a wish!

_____ **7.** Some people believe that thirteen is an unlucky number.

_____ **8.** Friday the thirteenth is a day that they believe brings misfortune.

_____ **9.** A horseshoe is what some people keep for good luck.

_____ **10.** Don't hang it with its prongs down, however, because the luck will spill out!

WORKSHEET 5 | Test (Rules 7 a–f)

EXERCISE A In each of the following sentences, underline each subordinate clause
and identify it on the line provided as *ADJ* (adjective), *ADV* (adverb), or *N* (noun).

EXAMPLE ___ADJ___ **1.** There is the dog <u>that is eating the cat's food</u>.

_____ **1.** Davis is the clerk who gave us the 50 percent discount on the shirts.

_____ **2.** We can go wherever you want for dinner.

_____ **3.** That the Nez Perce lived in Washington is true.

_____ **4.** What Aaron did for his parents was wonderful!

_____ **5.** Where is the key that will unlock the cabinet?

_____ **6.** The committee gave whoever ran in the race a free T-shirt.

_____ **7.** Here are the Japanese gardens we heard about last spring.

_____ **8.** Whoever wins the contest will receive a substantial cash prize.

_____ **9.** The orange crop will be good this year unless there is a late freeze.

_____ **10.** The swimming instructor who taught me the backstroke is returning
this year.

_____ **11.** When the whippoorwill starts singing, winter is over in our town.

_____ **12.** I acted as if I knew the ending of the movie.

_____ **13.** Sheri liked the dress that Alicia wore to the party.

_____ **14.** My boyfriend is the one who wrote that song.

_____ **15.** The referee announced who was penalized.

_____ **16.** The assignment is that we read another Paul Laurence Dunbar poem.

_____ **17.** The crowd applauded loudly for whoever played last.

_____ **18.** We stood while the rabbi read from the Torah.

_____ **19.** She is the debater whose arguments are most intelligent.

_____ **20.** Because the air conditioner is broken, we opened all the windows.

_____ **21.** The Romans believed that odd numbers were powerful.

_____ **22.** Because it is heavy, cold air hovers near the earth.

_____ **23.** The Druids believed that mistletoe is the antidote to all poisons.

_____ **24.** Although I have read about weather patterns, I want to know more.

_____ **25.** The brush that Will used for painting is soaking in a cleaning solution.

Continued ☞

EXERCISE B   In each of the following sentences, underline the two subordinate clauses. In the space above each subordinate clause, identify the clause by writing *ADJ* for adjective clause, *ADV* for adverb clause, or *N* for noun clause.

                     ADV   *ADJ*

EXAMPLE 1. <u>If you see Nancy</u>, ask her about the books <u>that I gave her</u>.

1. If you like magic realism, read something by Gabriel García Márquez, who often uses that technique.

2. Since we have no practice room, we have dropped varsity wrestling, which has always been a popular sport.

3. What I asked for was a book that had a poem by Mari Evans in it.

4. The losses that they suffered in the stock market were losses all brokers expect.

5. When he opened the mail, he found the letter that he had been looking for.

6. Wherever you go, you will find people who are interesting.

7. If you like to write, include a course in creative writing among those that you elect.

8. Don't repeat what she said, because she does not want to be quoted.

9. I was offered the job I wanted, and my parents, who have always been supportive of me, were thrilled.

10. Although Spencer plays lacrosse, he did not know that the game originated with the Indians of Canada.

EXERCISE C   On the line provided, identify each of the following clauses as *I* for independent or *S* for subordinate.

            EXAMPLE ____*I*____ **1.** We watered the yard every week.

_____ 1. Where the barrio begins.

_____ 2. Cicadas flew into our faces.

_____ 3. What the coach said.

_____ 4. Which chewed up the telephone book.

_____ 5. Whose name is on the check.

_____ 6. That really is a funny story.

_____ 7. Since we enjoy science fiction movies.

_____ 8. Mr. Baxter hired me.

_____ 9. Whoever plays the mandolin.

_____ 10. Which student has the most points?

| WORSHEET 1 | **Identifying Sentences and Sentence Fragments (Rule 8 a)** |

EXERCISE A   Decide whether each of the following word groups is a sentence or a sentence fragment. *Remember:* A sentence contains a subject and a verb and expresses a complete thought. If the word group is a sentence, write *S* on the line provided. If it is a sentence fragment, write *F*.

EXAMPLES ___F___ **1.** Because canoeing can be dangerous.

___S___ **2.** A canoeist should learn proper technique and safety rules.

_____ **1.** Taking a canoe trip in Canada.

_____ **2.** Sufficient food for a week's journey.

_____ **3.** Others had camped there before us.

_____ **4.** Ashes indicated the place.

_____ **5.** Where their fire had been.

_____ **6.** How clearly was the trail marked?

_____ **7.** An Ojibwa village at the end of the trail.

_____ **8.** The group spent the morning together.

_____ **9.** Talking over plans for the afternoon.

_____ **10.** As we rounded a bend in the river.

_____ **11.** Could you hear the noise of the waterfall?

_____ **12.** Before you could see it.

_____ **13.** We could not paddle against the wind unless the guide helped us.

_____ **14.** The wind blowing spray over us.

_____ **15.** Drenched to the skin.

_____ **16.** The rapids in the river were occasional hazards.

_____ **17.** The excitement of shooting the rapids.

_____ **18.** We steered and balanced carefully.

_____ **19.** Around boulders in the stream.

_____ **20.** Deciding whether to go through the rapids or portage the canoe around them.

_____ **21.** On our knees in the canoe, we became painfully cramped.

_____ **22.** There was no chance, however, to stretch our legs.

_____ **23.** From the beginning of the rapids to the end.

Continued ☞

LANGUAGE HANDBOOK **8** **WORKSHEET 1** *(continued)*

_____ **24.** Grazing the side of the canoe on rounded boulders.

_____ **25.** After we had taken a swim in the calm water beyond the rapids.

EXERCISE B Decide whether each of the following groups of words is a sentence or a sentence fragment. If the word group is a sentence, underline the subject once and the verb twice, and write *S* for sentence on the line provided. If the subject *you* is understood, write *you* in parentheses at the end of the item. If the word group is a sentence fragment, write *F* for fragment.

EXAMPLES _____S_____ **1.** The <u>director</u> <u><u>is looking</u></u> for talented, hard-working performers.

_____F_____ **2.** Kneeling near the edge of the stage.

_____S_____ **3.** <u><u>Raise</u></u> the curtain. (*you*)

_____ **1.** The audience moved by his dramatic performance.

_____ **2.** Mrs. Linares, the director of this classic tragedy.

_____ **3.** Near the end of the first act.

_____ **4.** Was playing the part of Lady Macbeth.

_____ **5.** Walking aimlessly about and rubbing her hands.

_____ **6.** At the final curtain came a loud burst of applause.

_____ **7.** The actors staying in character during five curtain calls.

_____ **8.** The most successful performance of the season.

_____ **9.** What is the director planning next?

_____ **10.** In the spring she will direct the well-known musical *West Side Story*.

_____ **11.** That story based on *Romeo and Juliet?*

_____ **12.** Are you interested in musicals?

_____ **13.** Hoping for the role of Bernardo?

_____ **14.** Practice the part now, and memorize the lines in time for the audition.

_____ **15.** Who will play Maria?

_____ **16.** A production of the play on public television.

_____ **17.** The necessity of a good cast.

_____ **18.** Although many of the songs from *West Side Story* have become famous.

_____ **19.** The performers must act, sing, and dance well.

_____ **20.** A very difficult and trying task for inexperienced actors.

LANGUAGE
HANDBOOK **8** SENTENCE STRUCTURE

| WORKSHEET 2 | ## Identifying and Using Subjects and Predicates (Rule 8 b) |

EXERCISE A For each of the following sentences, underline the complete subject once and the complete predicate twice.

> **EXAMPLE 1.** <u>Stanislaw Lem</u> <u>wrote the science fiction novel *Solaris*</u>.

1. I frequently daydream about the future.

2. The achievements of scientists will change our lives.

3. Education will undoubtedly benefit from scientific progress.

4. Teaching machines may someday replace classroom lectures.

5. Software programs have already taught important facts to students.

6. Hypnotism could revolutionize teaching procedures.

7. Some other speculations are even more interesting.

8. Scientists may one day be able to freeze a person alive.

9. This person might be revived after decades of the deep-freeze treatment.

10. Today's science fiction often becomes tomorrow's reality.

EXERCISE B The following groups of words are not sentences. In some of them the subject is missing; in others, the predicate is missing. For each group of words, make up the missing part and write it on the lines provided.

> **EXAMPLE 1.** Special events held in the classroom <u>can be both fun and educational.</u>

1. _____

decided to have an international luncheon in honor of United Nations Day.

2. _____

decorated their classroom with flags from other countries.

3. Many friends and relatives _____

_____

4. _____

brought some crisp banana chips.

5. Souvlaki and other foods from Greece _____

_____

LANGUAGE
HANDBOOK **8** **SENTENCE STRUCTURE**

| WORSHEET 3 | **Identifying the Simple Subject and the Simple Predicate (Rules 8 c, d, g)** |

EXERCISE A In each of the following sentences, circle the simple subject and underline the simple predicate, or verb.

> **EXAMPLE** 1. A new (bridge) across the Chippewa River <u>was built</u> last summer.

1. The town's water pipe was in the way of the new bridge.
2. What solution did the town adopt?
3. There was space for a new pipe along the underside of the bridge.
4. Last night brought the coldest weather in ten years.
5. At three o'clock in the morning the town was awakened by the fire siren.
6. In the center of town a big house was blazing.
7. The fire hoses were useless.
8. The water had frozen in the exposed pipe under the bridge.
9. The house was owned by the construction engineer for the new bridge.
10. The poor man's mistake had come home to roost.

EXERCISE B In each of the following sentences, circle the simple subject and underline the simple predicate, or verb. If the subject is the understood *you,* write *you* in parentheses after the sentence. Include all parts of a verb phrase.

> **EXAMPLES** 1. (Each) of the men <u>will help</u>.
> 2. Please <u>sit</u> down. ((you))

1. Do you like humorous fiction?
2. Read James Thurber's stories.
3. His funny stories are full of peculiar people and animals.
4. One of Thurber's aunts is always throwing shoes during the night.
5. The cause of this action is her fear of imaginary burglars.
6. How does a cousin in this story act at night?
7. Every hour he wakes up breathless.
8. What are Thurber's dogs doing?
9. One of his dogs bites at the air near panic-stricken guests.
10. Other dogs are even stranger!

LANGUAGE HANDBOOK 8 SENTENCE STRUCTURE

WORKSHEET 4 | Identifying the Simple Subject and the Simple Predicate (Rules 8 c, d–g)

EXERCISE A   In each of the following sentences, circle the simple subject and underline the simple predicate, or verb. If the subject is the understood *you,* write *you* in parentheses after the sentence.

> EXAMPLES 1. How <u>can</u> (humans) <u>help</u> to save endangered species?
>
> 2. <u>Carry</u> the chair into the other room. ((you))

1. The Korean martial art of tae kwon do has become internationally popular.

2. Do earthquakes cause tidal waves?

3. Please help Pedro with those boxes.

4. How does a hibernating animal avoid starvation?

5. Mr. Talbot plays the sitar, an instrument from India.

6. Helena Rubinstein built a profitable cosmetics empire.

7. One spring there was a violent tornado in Illinois.

8. There are many differences between an alligator and a crocodile.

9. The telephone wires were severely damaged by the storm.

10. In Mrs. Kim's purse were some valuable papers.

EXERCISE B   In each of the following sentences, circle the simple subject and underline the simple predicate, or verb. If the subject is the understood *you,* write *you* in parentheses after the sentence. Include all parts of a compound subject, a compound verb, or a verb phrase.

> EXAMPLE 1. (Brett) and (Eartha) <u>will</u> probably <u>win</u> the election.

1. In Ms. Thomas's class, we are studying the works of Sandra Cisneros.

2. Do any animals thrive in Death Valley?

3. Parasol ants raise their own crop of mushrooms.

4. What does this signal mean to an airplane pilot?

5. Boys and girls busily washed the dishes and cleaned the house.

6. One of the modern poets is Gwendolyn Brooks.

7. Have the police been notified yet?

8. Did you or she write and send this note?

9. By how much did the committee underestimate our expenses?

10. Open the box and look inside.

WORKSHEET 5 | Identifying the Simple Predicate (Rule 8 d)

EXERCISE A Draw a line under the complete predicate and a circle around the simple predicate, or verb, in each of the following sentences. If the parts of a verb are separated, be sure to circle each part.

EXAMPLE 1. The moon (will) then (pass) between the earth and the sun.

1. Mexican mariachi bands usually include violins, guitars, and trumpets.

2. Your help has always been valuable to me.

3. Worst of all is the multiple-choice spelling test.

4. Sea urchins have many movable spines.

5. August Wilson's play *The Piano Lesson* is set in the 1930s.

6. Did the burglar have a key to the store?

7. The surgeon did not recommend an immediate operation.

8. Is the pilot light of the furnace still burning?

9. Have you ever heard of a Caesar salad?

10. A diet limited to proteins and fats would actually starve a rat to death.

EXERCISE B Underline the simple predicate, or verb, in each of the following sentences. Be sure to include all parts of a verb phrase.

EXAMPLE 1. I <u>have</u> always <u>enjoyed</u> reading mythical stories.

1. Folk tales and legends have filled the world with imaginary creatures.

2. Many of these creatures are composed of parts of various real animals.

3. The mythical manticore had the face of a man, the body of a lion, and the tail of a scorpion.

4. This powerful beast could run very fast.

5. According to legend, the manticore would devour a person with its three rows of teeth.

6. A glance at Medusa could also be a fatal occurrence.

7. Medusa, a creature with a woman's body and face, grew snakes from her head as hair.

8. One look at Medusa's face would turn unlucky viewers into stone.

9. The griffin was formed from the head and wings of an eagle and the body of a lion.

10. The Chimera is commonly pictured with the head of a lion, the body of a goat, and the tail of a serpent.

LANGUAGE HANDBOOK 8 SENTENCE STRUCTURE

WORKSHEET 6 | Identifying Compound Subjects and Compound Verbs (Rules 8 e, f)

EXERCISE Each of the following sentences has a compound subject, a compound verb, or both a compound subject and a compound verb. Underline each compound subject once and each compound verb twice.

> EXAMPLES 1. <u>Punch</u> and <u>Judy</u> are popular puppets.
>
> 2. People <u>laugh</u> and <u>applaud</u> during the puppet shows.

1. Toni Cade Bambara taught in colleges, wrote fiction, danced, and did social work.

2. The Sirens, Circe, and the goddess Calypso all tempted Odysseus and his men.

3. At the airport, my aunt and uncle checked their baggage and ran to their gate.

4. Jack London quit school at age fourteen but later attended a year of college at age twenty.

5. *Firefly* and *lightning bug* are two names for the same winged beetle.

6. Chief Joseph of the Nez Perce tried but failed to keep his people's homeland.

7. While Chief Joseph's troops fought the U.S. Army, the Nez Perce women and children were well protected.

8. Chief Joseph's ideas and eloquent speech are greatly admired now.

9. Travel and adventure filled Mark Twain's life as a steamboat pilot on the Mississippi River.

10. Pine, spruce, and fir are kinds of cone-bearing evergreen trees.

11. The teacher and his class looked through the textbook and decided to read the *Odyssey*.

12. Many people have climbed, written about, and photographed Mount Everest.

13. While at such high elevations, most people carry and use supplemental oxygen.

14. Some Sherpas and a few other climbers are able to reach the top of the mountain without using extra oxygen.

15. Climbers carefully prepare and practice before attempting to reach Mount Everest's 29,028-foot summit.

16. Other members of the Sports Club and I appreciate and enjoy books and films about Mount Everest.

17. However, neither I nor my friends plan to attempt the climb any time soon.

18. The dog next door barks, whines, and howls every night.

19. Maybe he needs company or is hungry.

20. Maybe he and his owner are bored with a quiet neighborhood.

LANGUAGE HANDBOOK 8 SENTENCE STRUCTURE

| WORSHEET 7 | Identifying Subject Complements and Direct Objects (Rules 8 h–j) |

EXERCISE A In each of the following sentences, underline the subject complement. Then, draw an arrow from the complement to the subject to which it refers. A sentence may have more than one subject complement. Some of the sentences do not have any subject complements.

EXAMPLE **1.** The tombs of Egyptian pharaohs were great <u>finds</u>.

1. In ancient Egypt, a tomb was not just a place to bury a body.

2. For the Egyptians, death was a continuation of life.

3. The tombs of Egyptian royalty were often very grand and should have been sacred.

4. Some of the tomb's contents were food and equipment for the deceased to use in the afterlife.

5. The tombs were sealed off from intruders.

6. The treasures in the tombs were irresistible to thieves.

7. Plundering became a frequent occurrence.

8. To robbers, a new royal tomb seemed an invitation for theft.

9. Many of those fabulous treasures might be found in museums today.

10. Only a few of the tombs were left undisturbed.

EXERCISE B Underline the subject of each sentence once and the verb twice. Then, draw an arrow from the verb to the direct object. A sentence may have more than one direct object.

EXAMPLES **1.** <u>Louise</u> <u><u>misspelled</u></u> ten words on the test.

2. Her failure <u>she</u> <u><u>attributed</u></u> to her lack of sleep.

1. Tyrone has already solved the first problem.

2. Last night's hail greatly damaged crops in this area.

3. The Pomo sometimes decorated their baskets with shells and feathers.

4. Four workers lifted the piano onto the stage.

5. The class elected two boys and two girls.

6. Lulu has trained her puppy to sit.

7. The huge crowd pushed Sean and me into the wrong bus.

8. Allen brought home a book about Leontyne Price.

9. The outfielder quickly threw the ball to home plate.

10. Heavy armor protects the armadillo.

WORKSHEET 8 | **Identifying Subject Complements, Direct Objects, and Indirect Objects (Rules 8 h–k)**

EXERCISE A   Underline each complement in the following sentences. Then, on the line provided, write *DO* if the complement is a direct object, *PN* if it is a predicate nominative, or *PA* if it is a predicate adjective.

> EXAMPLES   __PN__   **1.** A craft fair is an excellent <u>idea</u>.
>
>   __DO__   **2.** We could raise <u>money</u> at a craft fair.
>
>   __PA__   **3.** The film was very <u>exciting</u>.

_____ **1.** The freshman class planned a craft fair.

_____ **2.** Some of their handcrafted objects were beautiful.

_____ **3.** The class would donate the proceeds to a local charity for the holiday season.

_____ **4.** Manuela asked several restaurant owners for empty bottles.

_____ **5.** Her collection was an interesting assortment of bottles in many shapes, sizes, and colors.

_____ **6.** Manuela carefully cut the top off each of the bottles.

_____ **7.** Then she sanded the rough edges.

_____ **8.** The old bottles became beautiful vases.

_____ **9.** One green bottle with a rounded bottom was especially attractive.

_____ **10.** This bottle became Manuela's best vase.

EXERCISE B   In the following sentences, underline each direct object once and each indirect object twice. You will not find an indirect object in every sentence.

> EXAMPLE **1.** The event gave <u>Roger</u> an <u>inspiration</u> for a story.

1. He sold Alvin a red sweater.

2. Bring me the book about Navajo blankets.

3. I'll give the receipt for the money to Helen.

4. The caller left you this message.

5. I threw Carmen the ball.

6. Has he read his students these stories?

7. Someone must have criticized his methods.

8. Dr. Mabie is leaving her college a valuable collection of old manuscripts.

9. Should I give the baby a bagel?

10. Shall I get the Wynton Marsalis CD for you?

8 SENTENCE STRUCTURE

WORKSHEET 9 **Classifying Sentences by Purpose and Structure (Rules 8 l, m)**

EXERCISE A On the line provided, identify each of the following sentences as declarative (*DEC*), imperative (*IMP*), interrogative (*INT*), or exclamatory (*EXC*). Then, add the necessary punctuation.

EXAMPLE _____DEC_____ **1.** Physics is a fascinating science.

_____ **1.** I read the book *Surely You're Joking, Mr. Feynman!* last month

_____ **2.** It is filled with funny anecdotes about physicist Richard Feynman's life

_____ **3.** Feynman worked with Edward Teller and knew Albert Einstein

_____ **4.** The reader has to laugh at the jokes Feynman played on people

_____ **5.** What fun he had

_____ **6.** Two of the smallest independent countries in the world are within Italy

_____ **7.** Do you know what they are

_____ **8.** Look them up in an encyclopedia

_____ **9.** One is Vatican City, and it has its own postal service and stamps

_____ **10.** How beautiful the other country, San Marino, is

EXERCISE B On the line provided, classify each of the following sentences as *S* for simple, *CD* for compound, *CX* for complex, or *CD-CX* for compound-complex.

EXAMPLE _____S_____ **1.** Some animals can seem to disappear.

_____ **1.** Many animals change color with the seasons, but some have the ability to change color instantly.

_____ **2.** Chameleons are lizards that can change to the color of the surface where they rest, whether it is black, red, yellow, white, or orange.

_____ **3.** Snowshoe hares are brown in the summer and white in the winter.

_____ **4.** Polar bears don't change colors but are camouflaged by their white fur.

_____ **5.** Many insects look like the branches on which they live.

_____ **6.** Grasshoppers usually become the color of whatever they eat.

_____ **7.** The flower mantis looks like a flower to attract the insects on which it feeds.

_____ **8.** Walking sticks are insects that look like twigs, and their appearance protects them from being eaten by birds.

_____ **9.** Baby animals are usually protected by their coloring.

_____ **10.** Fawns, for example, are dappled like the forest floor when they are young and later become evenly brown, the color of tree trunks.

LANGUAGE HANDBOOK 8 SENTENCE STRUCTURE

WORKSHEET 10 Test (Rules 8 a–m)

EXERCISE A In each of the following sentences, circle the simple subject and underline the simple predicate, or verb. If the subject is the understood *you*, write *you* in parentheses after the sentence. Be sure to include all parts of a verb phrase and all parts of a compound subject or verb.

EXAMPLES 1. <u>Are</u> (all) of the boys <u>working</u>?

2. Please <u>pick</u> up the book and <u>bring</u> it here. ((you))

3. (Darlene) and (Trent) <u>are bringing</u> the bread and the tomatoes to the potluck supper.

1. Pam and she made the egg rolls.

2. Did any of the cups break?

3. There is a beautiful kimono displayed in Mrs. Ozawa's house.

4. Do not tell me the answer yet.

5. Here is a copy of Denise Chávez's new play.

6. None of the food was edible.

7. What could he have been doing?

8. Under the bridge was quicksand.

9. Has either of you seen Elena?

10. I read Leslie Marmon Silko's story and then wrote my paper.

11. Both of the twins are talented.

12. You and she are the favorites.

13. Has the bell rung?

14. I mailed the letter on Monday and received a reply on Friday.

15. How did you like the play?

16. Beyond the lake are mountains.

17. I washed and dried the dishes.

18. Read the story "Independence" by Ruth Sasaki.

19. How beautiful the sunset is!

20. When will you visit the Museum of Indian Arts and Culture in New Mexico?

Continued ☞

EXERCISE B Each of the following sentences has either a compound subject or a compound verb. Underline each compound subject once and each compound verb twice.

> EXAMPLES 1. Five baby rabbits <u>romped</u> and <u>played</u> in the yard.
>
> 2. Neither our <u>dog</u> nor our <u>cat</u> bothered them.

1. In Aristotle's theory, fire, air, water, and earth make up all matter.

2. Aristotle weighted and ranked the elements in that order, from lightest to heaviest.

3. To him, the properties and movements of objects were determined by these elements.

4. The spirit and humor of Harold Krents are evident in his writing.

5. His autobiography, *To Race the Wind*, relates his experiences and describes his blindness.

6. Despite his lack of vision, Krents ran, played, went to school, and became an attorney.

7. Krents's healthy outlook and sense of humor inspired playwright Leonard Gershe's book *Butterflies Are Free.*

8. Mandan, Dakota, Crow, and Osage are some of many Sioux languages.

9. In Mexico, Porfirio Díaz fought and served as general, statesman, and president.

10. Some cutting tools, phonograph needles, and abrasives come from diamonds.

EXERCISE C In the following sentences, underline each complement. Then, in the space above each underlined complement, write the abbreviation that correctly identifies the complement. Write *PN* for predicate nominative, *PA* for predicate adjective, *DO* for direct object, or *IO* for indirect object.

> ⠀⠀⠀⠀⠀⠀⠀⠀⠀*IO*⠀⠀⠀*DO*
> EXAMPLE 1. Ants caused <u>me</u> <u>trouble</u> in my back yard.

1. They taught me the meaning of persistence.

2. I often watched the ants at work.

3. I watered the lawn every day after school.

4. This chore became interesting work for me.

5. I flooded a huge anthill with water.

6. I thus declared war on the colony of ants.

7. Perhaps ants are more intelligent than we think.

8. Their subsequent actions seemed sensible.

9. These ants were unusually crafty.

10. In fact, they appeared smarter than me.

Continued ☞

EXERCISE D The complements in the following sentences are in italics. In the space above each complement, identify the complement by writing *PN* for predicate nominative, *PA* for predicate adjective, *DO* for direct object, or *IO* for indirect object.

                                                                        DO
> **EXAMPLE 1.** Tales of Sasquatch, or Bigfoot, intrigued *me* throughout my childhood in the Pacific Northwest.

1. Several people traveled the mountain *trails* and brought *tales* back from their trips.

2. Some of these tales seemed *incredible*.

3. One camper told *me* a strange *story*.

4. While hiking in the backwoods, she saw large *footprints* ahead of her on the trail.

5. They appeared too *large* to belong to a human.

6. She made plaster *casts* of the footprints and gave an *anthropologist* the *casts*.

7. The unknown walker must have been a large *creature*.

8. Probably five hundred pounds was its *weight* and eight feet was its *height*.

9. It had a long, flat-footed *gait*.

10. Is the creature Bigfoot a *myth*, or is it a *reality*?

EXERCISE E For each item below, write an original sentence in the specified word order. Add modifiers when needed. Circle the required parts in your sentences.

> **EXAMPLE 1.** Subject—verb—direct object
> The (waiter) then (served) the (soup.)

1. Subject—verb—direct object _____

_____

2. Subject—verb—indirect object—direct object _____

_____

3. Verb—subject—predicate nominative _____

_____

4. Subject—verb—indirect object—direct object _____

_____

5. Subject—verb—predicate adjective _____

_____

Continued ☞

EXERCISE F   On the line provided, identify each of the following sentences as declarative (*DEC*), imperative (*IMP*), interrogative (*INT*), or exclamatory (*EXC*). Then, add the necessary punctuation.

EXAMPLE ___INT___ **1.** Who is your hero or heroine**?**

_____ **1.** Don't forget to read Dr. Martin Luther King, Jr.'s, speeches

_____ **2.** Wow, he was a great man

_____ **3.** Have you heard recordings of any of his talks

_____ **4.** His voice was expressive and his language was eloquent

_____ **5.** Have you ever taken a photography class

_____ **6.** One wildlife photography class meets at the city park

_____ **7.** Do you think of the animals in the park as wildlife

_____ **8.** In Florida it's possible to photograph wildlife near any pond

_____ **9.** Don't step too close to the alligators

_____ **10.** Work quietly so that the birds do not fly away

EXERCISE G   On the lines provided, classify the following sentences as *S* for simple, *CD* for compound, *CX* for complex, or *CD-CX* for compound-complex.

EXAMPLE ___S___ **1.** We enjoy art class projects.

_____ **1.** The art club is sponsoring a multicultural festival that will be held in March.

_____ **2.** Our class is working with papier-mâché to make piñatas, and many students are creating wonderful figures.

_____ **3.** We bought candles, paper bags, and sand to use for lanterns, which will light the path to the gym where the festival will be held.

_____ **4.** John and Charley, who are brothers, are making drums that they will play.

_____ **5.** Tanya and Chloe are designing a mural depicting African heritage.

_____ **6.** When the design is finished, many of the students will help with the painting.

_____ **7.** Bright Chinese lanterns are being hung between banners made of silk.

_____ **8.** Colorful table runners that show family histories are being painted by students, and centerpieces are being made by the ceramics class.

_____ **9.** Families will bring different ethnic foods for the festival.

_____ **10.** The festival is popular, and we hope that this art class tradition continues.

WORKSHEET 1 | **Creating Sentences from Fragments (Rule 9 a)**

EXERCISE A On the lines provided, rewrite each fragment as a complete sentence.

EXAMPLE **1.** A display about fruit bats. _We saw a display about fruit bats._

1. Cleared the path. _____

2. Lost the car keys again. _____

3. Ran ten miles before breakfast. _____

4. Bought and sold coffee cups. _____

5. When the canoe overturned. _____

_____

6. The tepees of the Great Lakes region. _____

_____

7. The shoppers under the awning. _____

_____

8. Zithers, violins, harps, and other types of stringed instruments. _____

_____

9. The new film about shipwrecks. _____

_____

10. Only the experienced workers. _____

_____

11. Traveled south, from the Canadian border. _____

_____

12. According to ancient legend. _____

_____

13. Frances and James, lost in the forest. _____

_____

14. Watched our favorite movie with us. _____

_____

15. Seen near the sequoia forest. _____

_____

Continued ☞

16. You should have heard. _____

_____

17. Staples, pens, tablets, or erasers. _____

_____

18. Last night, most of the audience. _____

_____

19. As soon as the wind has stopped blowing. _____

_____

20. From Guanajuato, a state in central Mexico. _____

_____

EXERCISE B The paragraph below contains ten sentence fragments. Join each fragment to a sentence by crossing out the unnecessary period and by crossing out the incorrect capital letter and replacing it with a lowercase letter.

> **EXAMPLE** Clean-up Day has been an annual event at our school. ~~E~~ver *e*
> since it was introduced seven years ago.

At our school, everyone looks forward to Clean-up Day. Even though it means hard work for all of us. All ninth-grade classes are excused for the afternoon on Clean-up Day. Which is observed every spring. Members of the student council supervise the work. After they have met previously to decide the area for which each class will be responsible. Some students are equipped with rakes and spades. That are lent by trusting parents who are interested in the project. Trash baskets, wheelbarrows, bushel baskets, hedge clippers, and even lawn mowers are rushed into action. When the time for work arrives at the beginning of the sixth period. After Clean-up Day ninth-graders are naturally interested in keeping the grounds neat. Because they have worked hard to get them that way. Of course, they don't want to see them littered with paper. You don't dare throw a gum wrapper or a lunch bag anywhere but in the trash baskets. Unless you want to have trouble with ninth-graders. Almost everyone enjoys Clean-up Day. Probably because most of us like to get out of going to classes. There are always some loafers. Who are more interested in getting out of work than in helping. Even the loafers, however, get busy. When they see how seriously most of the students take the work.

LANGUAGE
HANDBOOK **9** **WRITING COMPLETE SENTENCES**

| **WORKSHEET 2** | **Revising Run-on Sentences (Rule 9 b)** |

EXERCISE A   On the lines provided, revise the following run-on sentences to make them correct. Use the method given in parentheses after each sentence.

> EXAMPLE   **1.** Dogs are barking they aren't ours. (*comma and coordinating conjunction*) _Dogs are barking, but they aren't ours._

1. Leonard gave an impromptu speech it actually sounded prepared. (*subordinate clause*) _____

_____

2. You can join us for supper you have to help with the dishes. (*semicolon and conjunctive adverb*) _____

_____

3. The *I Ching* is an ancient Chinese book, a copy is in the library. (*two sentences*) _____

_____

4. Francine is getting new glasses tomorrow her prescription is the same. (*semicolon and conjunctive adverb*) _____

_____

5. The art club is going to the exhibit of African masks I want to go. (*comma and coordinating conjunction*) _____

_____

6. The house has a mansard roof the place looks nice. (*semicolon*) _____

_____

7. My little sister is memorizing the multiplication table, she is a good student. (*subordinate clause*) _____

_____

8. Jake was removed from the hockey game he sat in the penalty box. (*two sentences*)

_____

9. That kind of pen is extremely handy I don't have one. (*comma and coordinating conjunction*) _____

_____

10. The election results have been counted the winner will be announced shortly. (*semicolon*) _____

_____

Continued ☞

LANGUAGE HANDBOOK **9** **WORKSHEET 2** *(continued)*

EXERCISE B On the lines provided, use a variety of methods to correct the run-on sentences in the following paragraph.

> **EXAMPLE** [1] I like to eat at my friend Juan's house his mother is a great cook.
>
> *I like to eat at my friend Juan's house. His mother is a great cook.*

[1] Her specialty is Mexican food that is my favorite. [2] No one makes guacamole the way she does she adds secret ingredients to the avocados. [3] I like her salsa her enchilada sauce is even better. [4] Both the salsa and sauce are spicy they aren't too hot to taste. [5] Juan's mother makes three kinds of enchiladas they are all good. [6] She'll serve your favorite kind you can sample all three. [7] I especially recommend the spinach enchiladas they are unusual. [8] I also enjoy her rice and beans, I always have large helpings. [9] The homemade tortillas are delicious I could eat them all day. [10] I always save room for flan for dessert it is the perfect way to end the meal.

WORKSHEET 3 **Test (Rules 9 a–b)**

EXERCISE A The following paragraphs contain some run-on sentences. On the lines provided, rewrite the paragraphs to correct the run-on sentences. *Note:* There may be more than one way to revise each run-on.

EXAMPLE A blizzard is a novelty in the South, many children have never seen a heavy snow.

A blizzard is a novelty in the South, where many children have ____
never seen a heavy snow. ____

Everyone at school was excited about the snow that fell yesterday in the classrooms teachers had difficulty keeping our attention. Of course, I, too, was very excited, as soon as school was out, I dashed home, put new film in my camera, and spent an hour taking snapshots. I took pictures at various angles of our new house to capture the beauty of the snow-laden shrubs, I also took several action shots of my dogs scuffling in deep drifts. Then, I snapped sparrows pecking at scraps of bread on the picnic table, which had deep snow on top of it, after building a snowman, I took a close-up of it, too.

Before I took the film to have the pictures developed, I remembered something, when I had snapped each picture, the camera had clicked, but the click had sounded unusual. Holding the unloaded camera up to the light, I pushed the button I heard the click but saw no flash of light. The shutter was not working, not one ray of light had reached the film!

_____

_____

_____

_____

_____

_____

_____

_____

_____

_____

_____

_____

_____

_____

Continued ☞

EXERCISE B The following story is confusing because it contains fragments and run-on sentences. Make the story clear by changing the punctuation and capital letters so that there will be no fragments or run-on sentences. Write your revision on the lines provided.

Captain Bill Atkins, a Brooklyn fisher, took his cruiser to the cod-fishing grounds off lightship *Ambrose* about 11:30 one morning last spring. Planning to catch a few cod. He baited some lines and tossed them over Harry, the only other member of the crew, busied himself in a similar manner. By the middle of the afternoon. They had collected a good catch. They had just decided to call it a day. When there came a huge tug on one of the lines. Indicating that an especially big one had taken the bait. Captain Atkins and Harry heaved mightily on the line. The fish finally broke above the surface, one look was enough for Harry. Who dropped the line and headed for the most remote spot on the boat. Near Captain Atkins lay a two-by-four. Which the undaunted captain seized in case he needed protection.

For a few moments the fish lay panting heavily on the deck. Giving Captain Atkins and Harry a chance to inspect it. This was the first time either man had ever seen such a monster. On its head were four horns and an antenna a foot long in its mouth, which was the size of a football, were five rows of vicious teeth the monster measured four-and-a-half feet in length and weighed seventy pounds while Harry and Captain Bill were gazing at this unknown caller, they were horror-struck when the "fish" shook off the effects of its hard landing and began to walk across the deck toward them. On its *feet!* Harry departed in haste Captain Atkins used his two-by-four to push the fish into the hold, where it would be confined, the bewildered captain turned his ship toward home.

The captain's fish story went the rounds in Brooklyn as fast as the captain could spread it about the details there could be no argument. Because, after all, there was the fish to be seen by anyone who wanted to see it, authorities at the American Museum of Natural History informed Captain Atkins that his monster was known by various names. The "angler fish" or the "goose fish" or the "fishing frog" fish of this kind usually do not swim but walk on the floor of the ocean. Waving their antennae to lure other fish Captain Atkins accepted this information, showing no interest in going to the bottom to get proof.

_____

_____

_____

_____

_____

_____

_____

_____

_____

_____

_____

Continued ☞

LANGUAGE HANDBOOK **10** **WRITING EFFECTIVE SENTENCES**

WORKSHEET 1 **Combining Sentences by Inserting Words and Phrases (Rules 10 a, b)**

EXERCISE A On the lines provided, combine each of the following sets of sentences by inserting a word or words from the second sentence into the first sentence. *Note:* There may be more than one way to combine each set. Add commas and change the forms of words where necessary.

EXAMPLES 1. The show's music has a loud beat. It is thumping. *The show's music has a loud, thumping beat.*

2. We were glad that we had studied for the exam. It was difficult. *We were glad the we had studied for the difficult exam.*

1. The pictures showed the rocky landscape. The landscape is Martian. _____

_____

2. An impala is a type of antelope. It is an African antelope. _____

_____

3. The doctors assured Roxy that she would walk again. They had much optimism. _____

_____

4. The apartment has high ceilings. The apartment is large. _____

_____

5. My parents prefer the music of the 1970s. They are old-fashioned. _____

_____

6. I want to study the culture of the Inuit. Their culture is fascinating. _____

_____

7. Carl was born in Alamogordo. Alamogordo is in New Mexico. _____

_____

8. Customers wanted more of the potato soup. The soup was peppery. _____

_____

9. The seats on the ride spin around. They spin quickly. _____

_____

10. The principal asks many questions. She likes to be helpful. _____

_____

Continued ☞

EXERCISE B   On the lines provided, combine each of the following pairs of sentences by taking a prepositional phrase from the second sentence and inserting it into the first. *Note:* There may be more than one correct way to combine each pair. You need to write only one revision.

> EXAMPLE **1.** Many Hopi live in Arizona.
>
> They live on the Hopi reservation there. *Many Hopi live on the Hopi reservation in Arizona.*

1. They live in villages.

The villages are on or near three high mesas. _____

_____

_____

_____

2. Hopi people have lived in pueblos.

They have lived in them for more than eight hundred years. _____

_____

_____

_____

3. The Hopi tend farms.

They tend farms in an extremely harsh climate. _____

_____

_____

_____

4. The Hopi spin and weave cotton into beautiful cloth.

The cotton is from their farms. _____

_____

_____

_____

5. An elderly woman rules a Hopi family.

She rules by tradition. _____

_____

_____

_____

| WORSHEET 2 | **Combining Sentences by Inserting Phrases (Rule 10 b)** |

EXERCISE A On the lines provided, combine each of the following pairs of sentences into one sentence. Take a phrase from one sentence, and insert it into the other sentence as an appositive phrase. Add commas if necessary. *Note:* There may be more than one correct way to combine each pair. You need to write only one revision.

EXAMPLE **1.** Blues music is usually sad in tone.

The music is a popular art form. *Blues music, a popular art form, is usually sad in tone.*

1. W. C. Handy published "Memphis Blues" in 1913.

He was one of the first blues musicians. _____

_____

_____

2. Handy also wrote "St. Louis Blues."

It is perhaps the most famous blues song. _____

_____

_____

3. Louis Armstrong was an innovative trumpeter.

He was a famous blues instrumentalist. _____

_____

_____

4. Bessie Smith's blues compositions made her famous during the 1920s.

They were simple songs full of power and beauty. _____

_____

_____

5. B. B. King continues the blues tradition.

He is a contemporary singer and composer. _____

_____

_____

Continued ☞

EXERCISE B On the lines provided, combine each of the following pairs of sentences into one sentence. Take a phrase from the second sentence and insert it into the first sentence as a participial phrase. Add commas if necessary.

> **EXAMPLE 1.** Many blues songs are popular.
>
> Many blues songs describe disappointments in love. *Many blues songs describing disappointments in love are popular.*

1. Blues music includes odd notes.

The notes are deliberately played out of tune. _____

_____

_____

2. Traditional blues lyrics consist of stanzas.

The stanzas contain three lines each. _____

_____

_____

3. "Memphis Blues" made blues music popular.

This song was written for a political campaign. _____

_____

_____

4. Blues music has strongly influenced many American composers.

These composers include George Gershwin. _____

_____

_____

5. Today there are many rock songs.

These songs reflect the influence of the blues. _____

_____

_____

LANGUAGE HANDBOOK **10** WRITING EFFECTIVE SENTENCES

WORKSHEET 3 | **Combining Sentences with Coordinating Conjunctions (Rule 10 c)**

EXERCISE On the lines provided, combine each of the following pairs of sentences by using a coordinating conjunction to create a compound subject or a compound verb. Be sure that the subject and verb agree in number in the combined sentence. You may also need to change other words. *Note:* There may be more than one correct way to combine each pair. You need to write only one revision.

EXAMPLES **1.** Jumping rope will raise your heart rate.

Running will raise your heart rate. _Jumping rope or running will raise your heart rate._

2. You should exercise every day.

You should eat right every day. _You should exercise and eat right every day._

1. Good diet is important for physical fitness.

Regular exercise is important for physical fitness. _____

_____

_____

2. You must exercise your muscles regularly.

You must stretch your muscles regularly. _____

_____

_____

3. Food is essential for your body.

Oxygen is essential for your body. _____

_____

_____

4. The heart helps distribute oxygen throughout the body.

The lungs help distribute oxygen throughout the body. _____

_____

_____

Continued ☞

5. Exercise makes the lungs more efficient.

It strengthens the heart. _____

_____

_____

_____

6. Swimming is an excellent form of exercise.

Jogging is an excellent form of exercise. _____

_____

_____

_____

7. Cycling every day conditions the body.

Walking every day conditions the body. _____

_____

_____

_____

8. Moderate exercise does not cause fatigue.

Moderate exercise does not damage the heart. _____

_____

_____

_____

9. Exercise helps you do more.

Exercise makes you feel less tired. _____

_____

_____

_____

10. You should begin an exercise program slowly.

You should build up gradually. _____

_____

_____

_____

| WORKSHEET 4 | **Combining Sentences and Using Parallel Structure (Rules 10 d, f)** |

EXERCISE A   On the lines provided, use coordinating conjunctions, semicolons, and conjunctive adverbs to combine each of the following pairs of sentences and create a compound sentence.

> **EXAMPLE 1.** The storm was ferocious. It was short. _The storm was_
> _ferocious; however, it was short._

1. The picture frame was too small. We trimmed the picture. _____

_____

2. I want to visit Peru one day. You can travel with me! _____

_____

3. The stained glass is dirty. It is still quite beautiful, however. _____

_____

4. Dad needs lots of help this summer. You can work for him. _____

_____

5. That song always makes me cry. I love to hear it. _____

_____

6. At first, our team's bobsled led the race. We were truly excited. _____

_____

_____

7. Two valves were burned on the car. Repair work was necessary immediately. _____

_____

_____

8. Only ten people attended the concert. They were enthusiastic. _____

_____

_____

9. The jasmine plant is a member of the olive family. Its flowers are highly fragrant. ____

_____

_____

10. Yoga is an ancient Hindu discipline. Many people still practice it today. _____

_____

_____

Continued ☞

EXERCISE B   On the lines provided, revise each of the following sentences by putting
the ideas in parallel form.

EXAMPLE   **1.** Mickey enjoys hiking and to snorkel. *Mickey enjoys hiking*
                   and snorkeling.

1. Confucius was a Chinese philosopher, and he also taught. _____

_____

2. Quickly, confidently, and with ease, the quarterback threw the ball. _____

_____

3. The squirrels in the yard receive food from not only us but also from our neighbors. __

_____

_____

4. Tomorrow I plan to weed the garden, to mow the yard, and some trimming. _____

_____

_____

5. The class favors holding a party and that school be dismissed early. _____

_____

_____

6. Sue and Tom hope to visit a mosque, and going to a synagogue is also something they
want to do. _____

_____

7. Always fair and because he has sympathy, Mr. Brown will be a good principal. _____

_____

_____

8. Going up the roller-coaster ramp wasn't too scary, but the trip down was frightening.

_____

_____

9. Gwen talked on the phone for two hours, and doing her homework took only twenty
minutes. _____

_____

10. The board voted to give Joanne a raise and increasing her hours. _____

_____

_____

| WORKSHEET 5 | **Combining Sentences with Adjective Clauses (Rule 10 e)** |

EXERCISE   On the lines provided, combine each of the following pairs of sentences. Change one sentence into an adjective clause and insert it into the other sentence to create a complex sentence. *Note:* There may be more than one correct way to revise each pair. You need to write only one revision.

EXAMPLE **1.** The sinking of the *Empress of Ireland* was a disaster.

This disaster caused the deaths of more than one thousand people. *The sinking of the Empress of Ireland was a disaster that caused the deaths of more than one thousand people.*

1. The ship was bound for London.

The ship set sail from Quebec on May 28, 1914. _____

_____

_____

2. The ship was traveling downstream.

The ship suddenly encountered a wispy fog near the mouth of the St. Lawrence River.

_____

_____

_____

3. The captain of the *Empress* spotted the lights of another ship.

The ship was passing nearby. _____

_____

_____

_____

4. The captain decided to change direction.

He had miscalculated the position of the other ship. _____

_____

_____

_____

Continued ☞

5. Tragically, the other ship changed its direction also.

This ship was called the *Storstad*. _____

_____

_____

_____

6. The freighter *Storstad* collided with the *Empress of Ireland*.

The *Storstad* could not decrease its momentum. _____

_____

_____

_____

7. The collision almost split the *Empress*.

The ship sank within fifteen minutes. _____

_____

_____

_____

8. On board the *Empress of Ireland* were many people.

They acted with great heroism. _____

_____

_____

_____

9. A passenger rescued a young girl by carrying her on his back.

She could not swim. _____

_____

_____

_____

10. One man had also survived the sinking of the ocean liner *Titanic*.

He was pulled from the water. _____

_____

_____

_____

LANGUAGE HANDBOOK 10 WRITING EFFECTIVE SENTENCES

WORKSHEET 6 | **Combining Sentences with Adverb Clauses (Rule 10 e)**

EXERCISE On the lines provided, combine each of the following pairs of sentences. Change one sentence into an adverb clause, and insert it into the other sentence to create a complex sentence. Add commas if necessary. *Note:* There may be more than one correct way to revise each pair. You need to write only one revision.

EXAMPLE 1. The Kwanzaa holiday nears its end.

The community gathers for a feast called *karamu*. *As the Kwanzaa holiday nears its end, the community gathers for a feast called karamu.*

1. The comedian entertained the audience.

   The stagehands changed the sets. _____

   _____

   _____

   _____

2. The assignment was difficult.

   Jules was able to finish in time. _____

   _____

   _____

   _____

3. Rosa does well in her audition.

   She may receive a part in the play. _____

   _____

   _____

   _____

4. The athletes began to practice the plays.

   The coach assigned the various positions. _____

   _____

   _____

   _____

Continued ☞

Elements of Literature

5. Salvador learned his routine well.

He coached the other members of the team. _____

_____

_____

_____

6. A hush fell upon the study hall.

The teacher walked into the room. _____

_____

_____

_____

7. Carla's group will not play at the dance.

The student government votes money to pay them. _____

_____

_____

_____

8. Lucy did her homework in the afternoon.

She wanted to go to the fair in the evening. _____

_____

_____

_____

9. Francisco was the best artist.

We asked him to draw the mural. _____

_____

_____

_____

10. Mr. Cohen sampled several different curries and chutneys.

He was traveling in India. _____

_____

_____

_____

LANGUAGE HANDBOOK **10** **WRITING EFFECTIVE SENTENCES**

| WORSHEET 7 | **Combining Sentences with Noun Clauses**
(Rule 10 e)

EXERCISE   On the lines provided, combine each of the following pairs of sentences. Change one sentence into a noun clause, and insert it into the other sentence to create a complex sentence. *Note:* There may be more than one correct way to revise each pair. You need to write only one revision.

EXAMPLES **1.** We now realize something about the Beatles.

The Beatles changed the course of popular music. *We now realize that the Beatles changed the course of popular music.*

2. Many teenagers prefer rock music to all other music.

This preference disturbs some adults. *That many teenagers prefer rock music to all other music disturbs some adults.*

1. The sushi chef told us something about the wasabi.

It is Japanese horseradish. _____

_____

2. Someone will win the trophy.

He will have the best batting average in the league. _____

_____

3. Why had the referee made that call?

The coach wanted to know. _____

_____

_____

4. We had put the car keys somewhere.

We could not remember. _____

_____

_____

_____

Continued ☞

5. The golfer's ball had gone somewhere.

The golfer could not discover where. _____

_____

_____

6. The actor told us something.

It was something we wanted to hear. _____

_____

_____

7. A person will buy this car.

That person will have to fix it. _____

_____

_____

8. Give the record to someone.

You decide upon the person. _____

_____

_____

_____

9. Solar cells work somehow.

How they work is baffling to me. _____

_____

_____

_____

10. I explained to Lucas.

The Koshare Indian Museum is in Colorado. _____

_____

_____

_____

Elements of Literature   *Writing Effective Sentences* **115**

LANGUAGE HANDBOOK 10 WRITING EFFECTIVE SENTENCES

| WORKSHEET 8 | **Revising Stringy and Wordy Sentences (Rules 10 g, h)** |

EXERCISE On the lines provided, revise the following stringy or wordy sentences to make them more concise.

EXAMPLE [1] The concert was fun, and it was enjoyable, and the tickets were affordable and at a good rate, too.

The concert was enjoyable. The tickets were affordable, too.

[1] The city's annual jazz concert, a yearly event, was held outdoors in the open air. [2] People came from everywhere for the concert, and they sat on blankets on the grass, and they brought their own refreshments and food and drinks. [3] The atmosphere and mood were festive and ebullient, and many bands entertained and singers joined them. [4] Throughout the concert there were various and diverse kinds of jazz played during the time. [5] The audience liked the music of Scott Joplin, and they appreciated John Coltrane's music, and Charlie Parker's music pleased them. [6] I myself think that I liked Joplin best. [7] A local singer from this area performed a tribute to Ella Fitzgerald, and Fitzgerald is widely admired, and it was great. [8] I've never heard jazz that was any better or that sounded superior. [9] I'm crazy about the saxophone, and several musicians played the sax, and I've studied it for years. [10] The concert was a huge success, and it made money and was a lucrative event, and I will return next year.

_____

_____

_____

_____

_____

_____

_____

_____

_____

_____

_____

_____

_____

_____

_____

_____

_____

_____

10 WRITING EFFECTIVE SENTENCES

| WORKSHEET 9 | **Varying Sentence Beginnings (Rule 10 i)** |

EXERCISE On the lines provided, vary the beginnings of sentences in the following paragraph. Other words may have to be added or changed.

EXAMPLE [1] A book editor reads many books in manuscript in order to consider them for publication.

In order to consider books for publication, a book editor reads
many manuscripts.

[1] A book editor is eager for new manuscripts and is always busy. [2] Manuscripts constantly pour into an editor's office, and the volume of material is amazing. [3] Editors receive many submissions these days as a result of home computers and desktop publishing systems. [4] Manuscripts vary a great deal, of course, in quality. [5] An editor can readily tell a good submission because of his or her training and natural ability. [6] An editor, not surprisingly, looks for strong writing, an interesting subject, and marketability. [7] He or she eliminates undesirable manuscripts with considerable speed. [8] The editor happily puts aside those manuscripts that seem special. [9] An editor negotiates with an author if he or she decides to accept a manuscript. [10] They agree mutually on contract terms, and the production process begins.

_____

_____

_____

_____

_____

_____

_____

_____

_____

_____

_____

_____

_____

_____

_____

EXERCISE A On the lines provided, rewrite each of the following short paragraphs by combining choppy sentences into longer, smoother sentences. Use your judgment about which sentences to combine and how to combine them.

EXAMPLE **1.** Stonehenge is in southern England. Stonehenge is the ruins of a monument. The monument is from the Neolithic period. People used this monument. They used it for performing religious rites. They used it for observing the stars. The monument contains a great circle of stone columns. The columns weigh more than 40 metric tons. The columns rise more than 7 meters above the ground.

Stonehenge, which is in southern England, is the ruins of a monument from the Neolithic period. People used this monument for performing religious rites and for observing the stars. The monument contains a great circle of stone columns. The columns weigh more than 40 metric tons and rise more than 7 meters above the ground.

1. Maxine Hong Kingston is an award-winning writer. She is the daughter of Chinese immigrants. She grew up in California. She was influenced by two cultures. The cultures were American and Chinese. Some of Kingston's stories feature Fa Mu Lan. Fa Mu Lan is a woman warrior. Her deeds depart from Chinese traditions.

_____

_____

_____

_____

_____

_____

2. Americans owe much to a Spanish governor of Louisiana. He was General Bernardo de Gálvez. He gave the Americans guns and supplies. He seized British warships. He did these things during the Revolutionary War. He tried to drive the British out of Louisiana. He finally took control of the entire area. This area was along the Gulf of Mexico. Americans were grateful. They named the city of Galveston in his honor.

_____

_____

_____

_____

_____

_____

Continued ☞

3. Nicholas Cugnot was a French artillery captain. He invented the automobile in 1770. It was the first successful automobile. The contraption was ugly. It had three wheels. The wheels were wooden. It resembled a large tricycle. A boiler produced steam. The boiler was coal-fired. The boiler was in front. The steam pushed two pistons. The pistons were on either side of the front wheel. The automobile moved at the speed of four kilometers per hour. This speed included time for stopping. The machine stopped every few hundred meters and regained steam pressure. The machine slipped on wet roads. The machine had steering problems. Cugnot's success inspired other daring inventors.

_____

_____

_____

_____

_____

_____

_____

_____

_____

EXERCISE B On the lines provided, revise each of the following sentences by putting the ideas in parallel form. Words may have to be added or changed.

EXAMPLE 1. Nicola and Carlo want to go to an amusement park on their vacation, and visiting the beach is also something they hope to do. *Nicola and Carlo want to go to an amusement park and visit the beach on their vacation.*

1. Ann likes to read poetry, but watching videos is also something she enjoys. _____

_____

2. Every weekend Mr. Liu sets aside some time to trim his rosebushes, watch a baseball game, and for reading to his grandson. _____

_____

3. My mother likes writing a weekly column for the local newspaper, and she is also a member of the city council. _____

_____

4. A fast runner and because she has a lot of energy, Robin should be a good addition to our soccer team. _____

_____

Continued ☞

5. The drive to Seattle didn't take too long, but coming back took five days. _____
_____

6. The doctor performed the emergency operation skillfully, quickly, and with
confidence. _____
_____

7. Tom bought his camping equipment from not only the local camping store but also
from a mail-order company. _____
_____

8. The chess club decided not only to have a tournament but opening it to anyone who
was interested. _____
_____

9. The voters in the last local election decided on lowering the sales tax and that the
park by the river be cleaned up. _____
_____

10. We decided both to watch a video and playing a board game. _____
_____

EXERCISE C   On the lines provided, revise the following stringy or wordy sentences.

EXAMPLE   [1] We went to our favorite bookstore, the one we like the best, to hear our
favorite author give a public reading for anyone who wanted to come.

We went to our favorite bookstore to hear our favorite author give a public
reading.

[1] All his fans came to hear him read, and they stood in line to buy copies of his
books, and some of them brought copies of his books from home that they had already
bought someplace else. [2] The bookstore manager seemed very satisfied and happy that
such a big crowd of the author's fans had turned out, and she made sure there were
enough copies of his books on display because she didn't want to run out of books for
people to buy. [3] When the author was ready to read, the manager announced him, and
all the people who had come to see the author read crowded into the seats that the
manager had set up ahead of time, and they all waited eagerly for the author to begin
reading from his new book. [4] The author read from his new collection of stories, and he
read from several of the stories, but not from all of them. [5] After the reading, when he
was finished, the author answered questions from the audience that was listening to him,
and the audience asked questions of the author about his life and his work. [6] Some of
the author's fans, who enjoy reading his books, asked him where he gets his ideas, and he
told them that he gets some of his ideas from stories that other people tell him, and he
told them that other ideas come from things he reads in the newspaper or sees on the
news on TV. [7] He also said that when he was in school, a teacher told him that he

Continued ☞

should write what he knows, but the writer said that when he was younger, he didn't think there was enough in his own personal experience for him to write about, and so he became comfortable with using his imagination and making things up. [8] After he had answered questions for half an hour, he sat down, and his readers lined up for him to sign his books, which he continued to do until all the people in the line were able to come up and get their books signed. [9] The line was very long, and it took a long time for the author to be able to sign all the books that his fans wanted him to sign. [10] When he had signed all the books of the people waiting in line, the author thanked the bookstore manager for asking him to come to the store and read from his books and sign copies of his books at her bookstore, and she said that she was very happy he was able to come because he was one of her favorite authors.

Continued ☞

EXERCISE D   On the lines provided, vary the beginnings of sentences in the following paragraph. Words may need to be added or changed.

> **EXAMPLE** [1] Odysseus had his men tie him to the mast of the ship so that he could hear the Sirens without harm.
>
> _So that he could hear the Sirens without harm, Odysseus had his men tie him to the mast of the ship._

[1] Odysseus left his home to fight at Troy, even though he was the king of Ithaca. [2] The Greeks had laid siege to the city of Troy because the Trojans had kidnapped Helen, the wife of the king of Sparta. [3] Odysseus and the Greeks all left Troy after the defeat of the Trojans in order to return to their homes. [4] Odysseus sailed for Ithaca with his ship and his crew. [5] He encountered along the way many adventures that slowed his journey home. [6] He encountered the Cyclops, for instance, a one-eyed giant who captured the crew of Odysseus and kept them in his cave. [7] The Cyclops was eating the men, one by one. [8] Odysseus and his men, in defense, blinded the Cyclops with a sharp stake. [9] Odysseus and his men sneaked out of the cave under the bellies of the Cyclops's sheep when the Cyclops could no longer see. [10] Odysseus went on to have many other adventures before he returned to Ithaca.

LANGUAGE HANDBOOK	**11**	**CAPITALIZATION**

WORKSHEET 1 | Capitalizing Words (Rules 11 a–f)

EXERCISE A   In the following letter, circle each lowercase letter that should be capitalized.

> **EXAMPLE** [1] I asked (m)ary, "(w)ould you give me some feedback about my theme paper?"

[1] dear mary,

[2] it was so nice to see you last weekend. [3] now I miss you again already, and, oh, how I wish you still lived in mayfield.

[4] thank you, o wise one, for your thoughtful comments about my paper on margaret walker's poem "lineage." [5] during my revisions, i've considered much of what you said. [6] for instance, I have placed more emphasis on the fact that walker repeats the line "my grandmothers were strong" three times.

[7] oh, by the way, I saw brian yesterday in my english class, and he said, "when is mary coming to visit again?" [8] we are all hoping the next visit will be soon.

> [9] your friend,

> [10] anna

EXERCISE B   In the following letter, circle each lowercase letter that should be capitalized.

> **EXAMPLE** [1] (p)eter asked (m)ason, "(w)hy can't I remember the name of that poem?"

[1] dear richard,

[2] do you think you could help me remember the title of a poem? [3] I've probably read the thing, oh, a dozen times, and yet I just can't think of the name of it. [4] I know you are familiar with this poem because it was in a book I borrowed from you once. [5] it begins, "in may, when sea winds pierced our solitudes." [6] another line I remember is "why thou wert there, o rival of the rose!" [7] if I'm not mistaken, it's by ralph waldo emerson. [8] your old friend is begging you, "please help!"

> [9] sincere thanks,

> [10] peter

Continued ☞

EXERCISE C   In the following items, draw a slanting line through errors in capitalization and write the letter correctly in the space above the error. If an item is already correct, write *C* on the line provided.

EXAMPLE _____   1. Kildare ~~r~~oad   *(R written above)*

_____   1. the Ohio river

_____   2. a Chicago firm

_____   3. Mount Katahdin

_____   4. Mecosta county residents

_____   5. the Rocky Mountains

_____   6. the atlantic ocean

_____   7. Pigeon river state forest

_____   8. great salt lake

_____   9. an ocean beach

_____   10. the pacific northwest

_____   11. the south side of nineteenth street

_____   12. the capital of north carolina

_____   13. San Diego county

_____   14. a new england village

_____   15. a lake michigan resort

_____   16. long island, new york

_____   17. crater lake national park

_____   18. chemistry II

_____   19. a city in the midwest

_____   20. the continents of Europe and Asia

_____   21. two miles east

_____   22. Main street runs north and south.

_____   23. an african country

_____   24. the gobi desert

_____   25. nations of the far east

LANGUAGE HANDBOOK 11 CAPITALIZATION

WORKSHEET 2 | Using Capitals for Proper Nouns, Proper Adjectives, and School Subjects (Rules 11 d–e)

EXERCISE A Change each proper noun below to a corresponding common noun. Change each common noun to a corresponding proper noun.

> **EXAMPLES** 1. Future Scientists' Club *a club for future scientists*
>
> 2. sometime next spring *on Thursday, May 14*

1. Parent-Teacher Association _____

2. a hospital in the city _____

3. the Civil War _____

4. algebra _____

5. a foreign language _____

EXERCISE B In the following paragraphs, draw a slanting line through each error in capitalization. Write your correction in the space above the error.

> **EXAMPLES** [1] Last fall during ~~t~~hanksgiving, Kim and her family took a
>
> ~~v~~acation in ~~f~~lorida. [2] They stayed at the King ~~h~~otel on
>
> Jackson Street.

[1] miami is probably the best-known resort in Florida, a popular vacation spot in the south. [2] Located at Florida's southern tip, Miami beach is actually a narrow island in the atlantic Ocean. [3] It is separated from the rest of Miami by Biscayne bay. [4] When tourists tire of sunning, they can visit the historic cape Florida Lighthouse, which was built in 1825. [5] People interested in art might enjoy a visit to the Dade county Art Museum, which was once the home of james Deering. [6] For nature enthusiasts, the Everglades National park is so rich in wildlife that a visit there in the summer is like an open-air classroom for nature 101.

[7] Other parts of Florida have attractions of their own. [8] For example, the Chassahowitzka National wildlife Refuge is near Homosassa. [9] The name of Lake okeechobee, located on the north end of the Everglades, is taken from a seminole word that means "big water." [10] Central Florida is known for its beautiful lakes and, of course, for Walt disney World.

LANGUAGE
HANDBOOK **11** **CAPITALIZATION**

| WORKSHEET 3 | ### Using Capitals for Proper Nouns, Proper Adjectives, School Subjects, and Titles (Rules 11 d–f) |

EXERCISE A   In the following paragraph, draw a slanting line through each error in capitalization and write the letter correctly in the space above the error.

>   *S*
> **EXAMPLE** [1] Reading mythology helps my S̸ister understand the origins
>   *E*
> of some Énglish words.

   [1] As an assignment for latin class, we read the tale of Orpheus and Eurydice in Robert Graves's book *the Greek myths.* [2] I enjoyed the story of the musician from thrace who charmed Hades, the God of the underworld, with his music. [3] The god was persuaded to allow Orpheus's Wife, Eurydice, to return to life. [4] But hades set one condition. [5] If Orpheus looked back to see whether his Wife was behind him before they both reached the upper world, Eurydice would have to return to the land of the dead. [6] On the brink of the upper world, the Master Musician looked back, and Eurydice was lost to him forever.

   [7] Our Teacher played parts of Gluck's opera *orpheus and eurydice.* [8] She arranged for us to obtain discount tickets to a film by the french director Jean Cocteau. [9] His film *orphée* was based on the ancient legend, which seems to have influenced many artists. [10] Last night, uncle Ernest showed me a print of the painting titled *Orpheus charming the beasts,* by a dutch artist.

EXERCISE B   On the line provided, write a brief sentence using each of the following capitalized and uncapitalized words correctly. Do not *begin* your sentence with the word given.

> **EXAMPLES** **1.** *General:* <u>The NATO commander was General Norstad.</u>
>   **2.** *general:* <u>Colin Powell is a general.</u>

1. *President:* _____

2. *president:* _____

3. *Mother:* _____

4. *mother:* _____

5. *aunt:* _____

| WORSHEET 4 | **Practicing Capital Letters (Rules 11 d–f)** |

EXERCISE A   Correct the following sentences by drawing a slanting line through each error in capitalization and writing the letter correctly in the space above the error.

> **EXAMPLE** **1.** Eva used ~~r~~omeo brand pasta and ~~j~~uliet olives in the ~~s~~alad she made for the ~~f~~ourth of July picnic.

1. Members of the baptist Training Union went as a group to see *The King of kings.* The Manager of the palace theater had made special arrangements for presenting this Classic during the easter holidays.

2. Today monuments erected by Historical Societies mark the oregon trail, which began at independence, missouri, and crossed kansas, nebraska, wyoming, idaho, and oregon.

3. Russell banks's *cloudsplitter* gives a vivid account of the attack on Harpers Ferry.

4. In 1862, president Lincoln issued the emancipation proclamation, officially freeing all the slaves in the confederacy on january 1, 1863.

5. Clara Barton was the First President of the american Red Cross.

6. Toni Morrison, a Professor at Princeton university, won a nobel prize because of her contributions to Literature; she is recognized especially for her novel *Beloved.*

7. Mrs. Kittridge explained that films such as *clueless* and *Great expectations* were based on Novels by Jane austen and Charles dickens.

8. Laura Bohannan, an american anthropologist, is best known for her study of the tiv people in West Africa.

9. *The Starry Night,* a painting by Vincent van Gogh, hangs in the museum of modern art in New York city.

10. Martin Luther King, Jr., who believed in nonviolent protest, was head of the Southern Christian leadership conference.

Continued ☞

EXERCISE B   In the following paragraphs, circle each lowercase letter that should be capitalized.

> **EXAMPLE** [1]   After we had finished reading selections from the divine comedy in english class last wednesday, ms. portinari asked us to write a composition.

[1] She said that most religions, from christianity to buddhism, include some concept of an afterlife. [2] Our assignment was to compare dante's idea of an afterlife with one found in another religion or in mythology. [3] I did my spanish and history assignments quickly and then spent most of the evening working on this task for english. [4] It was the most thought-provoking assignment I had had since entering martin luther king high school.

[5] I decided to investigate some ideas found in buddhism. [6] My aunt, who teaches a course in philosophy and religion at the university of hawaii in honolulu, told me that although buddhism is largely an Eastern religion, its ideas and dogmas are quite familiar to people living in the Western world. [7] This religion is an outgrowth of hinduism. [8] siddhartha Gautama received enlightenment after meditating under a tree at a place called Buddh Gaya. [9] Followers of buddhism believe that people experience a series of reincarnations. [10] According to aunt Sylvia, buddhists feel that people control their destinies. [11] The good or evil they do in this life controls the type of life they will have in their next reincarnation. [12] Since buddhists consider life to be full of suffering, their ultimate goal is to end this series of reincarnations. [13] The final state of blessedness is called *nirvana.*

[14] Actually, the ideas of Dante and the ideas of buddhists are very far apart. [15] While the italian master presented a world in which good and evil were rewarded or punished after death, the buddhists present a world in which people are compensated for their actions in their next lives. [16] In Dante's christian philosophy, the good are rewarded with paradise. [17] For buddhists, the good are rewarded by ceasing to exist.

[18] Last night father brought home a copy of a book by an austrian writer, heinrich harrer. [19] His book, *seven years in Tibet*, is about his life among tibetan buddhists. [20] Both mother and father saw a movie version of *seven years in tibet* last year at the beekman theater.

LANGUAGE HANDBOOK **11** CAPITALIZATION

WORKSHEET 5 | Test (Rules 11 a–f)

EXERCISE A For each of the following pairs of phrases, write the letter of the correctly capitalized phrase on the line provided.

EXAMPLE ___*a*___ 1. **a.** Seneca Lake   **b.** Seneca lake

_____ 1. **a.** the Virgin Islands   **b.** the Virgin islands

_____ 2. **a.** a State Park   **b.** a state park

_____ 3. **a.** the aim of the South   **b.** the aim of the south

_____ 4. **a.** a mile North of here   **b.** a mile north of here

_____ 5. **a.** the Vietnam Veterans Memorial   **b.** the Vietnam veterans memorial

_____ 6. **a.** a City in Guatemala   **b.** a city in Guatemala

_____ 7. **a.** the planet Saturn   **b.** the planet saturn

_____ 8. **a.** next Sunday   **b.** next sunday

_____ 9. **a.** next Spring   **b.** next spring

_____ 10. **a.** the Great Wall of China   **b.** the great wall of China

_____ 11. **a.** our English teacher   **b.** our english teacher

_____ 12. **a.** courses in Mathematics   **b.** courses in mathematics

_____ 13. **a.** taking Geometry I   **b.** taking geometry I

_____ 14. **a.** a Polynesian dance   **b.** a Polynesian Dance

_____ 15. **a.** Redlands High School   **b.** Redlands high school

_____ 16. **a.** Cable News Network   **b.** Cable News network

_____ 17. **a.** for my Father   **b.** for my father

_____ 18. **a.** the Polynesian Gods   **b.** the Polynesian gods

_____ 19. **a.** faith in God   **b.** faith in god

_____ 20. **a.** *The Diary of Anne Frank*   **b.** *the Diary of Anne Frank*

_____ 21. **a.** Twenty-First Street   **b.** Twenty-first Street

_____ 22. **a.** Woof-Woof dog food   **b.** woof-woof dog food

_____ 23. **a.** the President of the club   **b.** the president of the club

_____ 24. **a.** the U.S. President   **b.** the U.S. president

_____ 25. **a.** several Buddhists   **b.** several buddhists

Continued ☞

LANGUAGE HANDBOOK **11** **WORKSHEET 5** *(continued)*

EXERCISE B In each of the following sentences, draw a line through any incorrectly capitalized or lowercased words and write the word or words correctly on the line provided. If the sentence contains no errors in capitalization, write *C* on the line provided.

EXAMPLES   *physical sciences*   **1.** I am learning a great deal about the ~~Physical Sciences~~.

     Science   **2.** Mr. Kohler is my teacher for Earth ~~science~~ I.

_____ **1.** The title of Professor Katakura's speech was "the Importance of Erosion."

_____ **2.** He delivered it to new members of the Future Farmers of America.

_____ **3.** First, he showed us some pictures of the Grand Canyon.

_____ **4.** "The Colorado river has cut into these rocks," he said.

_____ **5.** He continued, "You High School students know this."

_____ **6.** then, he told us how water changes the land.

_____ **7.** The Mountains in New Hampshire show effects of erosion.

_____ **8.** Frozen water in the form of glaciers carved rounded passes called "notches" in the White mountains.

_____ **9.** Heavy Spring rains wash topsoil into rivers.

_____ **10.** Each week the Mississippi River carries millions of tons of land to the gulf of Mexico.

_____ **11.** That friday night my father and I went to the Tower Theater.

_____ **12.** On the screen, settlers were moving Westward.

_____ **13.** I was still thinking about the Professor's lecture.

_____ **14.** The story of early Western life did not interest me.

_____ **15.** I liked, however, scenes of the ocean and the rockies.

_____ **16.** "The Pacific ocean," I said, "is like an investor."

_____ **17.** later, my father asked me to explain my odd comparison.

_____ **18.** An investor puts money into a Company to make money.

_____ **19.** By evaporating, the ocean transfers water onto land.

_____ **20.** This water, or "principal," eventually returns to the Ocean and brings valuable minerals, or "interest."

LANGUAGE HANDBOOK **12** **PUNCTUATION**

| WORSHEET 1 | **Using End Marks (Rules 12 a–d)**

EXERCISE A   Place the appropriate end mark in the appropriate place in each of the following sentences.

EXAMPLE **1.** What did I say in my note to Celia**?**

1. I asked Celia what animal uses its nose for an arm

2. Celia's note to me had the correct answer and also said, "Try to stump me again"

3. Mr. Baker said, "Tell me why tears come to your eyes when you are peeling an onion"

4. After a moment, he asked, "What is the difference between an onion and an apple"

5. Stalling for time, Celia exclaimed, "An onion and an apple"

EXERCISE B   Change each of the following sentences into the type of sentence indicated by the word in italics, write the new sentence on the line provided, and supply the appropriate end mark. Add or omit words when necessary.

EXAMPLES   The game starts at two o'clock.

    1. *Interrogative:* _Does the game start at two o'clock_**?** _____

    2. *Imperative:* _Start the game at two o'clock_**.** _____

That fumble will cost us the game.

  1. *Interrogative:* _____

  2. *Exclamatory:* _____

Mario should leave at once.

  3. *Interrogative:* _____

  4. *Imperative:* _____

Was that road dangerous?

  5. *Declarative:* _____

  6. *Exclamatory:* _____

Cai told him what I said.

  7. *Interrogative:* _____

  8. *Exclamatory:* _____

The rug should be cleaned right away.

  9. *Interrogative:* _____

 10. *Imperative:* _____

LANGUAGE HANDBOOK **12** PUNCTUATION

WORKSHEET 2 — Punctuating Abbreviations; Using Commas in a Series (Rules 12 e, f)

EXERCISE A   Insert periods where they are needed in the following sentences. If a sentence does not require additional periods, write *C* on the line provided.

EXAMPLE _____ **1.** My sister works at Mrs. Miller's dry cleaning shop every Saturday from 8:00 A.M. till 4:00 P.M.

_____ **1.** The John F Kennedy Library, in Boston, Mass, was designed by the famous architect I M Pei.

_____ **2.** Mr Benally's new address is 1860 Vine St, Augusta, GA 30903.

_____ **3.** The Nok civilization flourished in West Africa from about 500 B C to about A D 200.

_____ **4.** Ms Powell now lives at 210 Fir Ave, Rapid City, SD 57701.

_____ **5.** The meeting will begin at 11:00 A M sharp and should be over by 12:30 P M.

_____ **6.** Dr. Kohari prescribed antibiotics for Mother's sinus infection.

_____ **7.** Sheryl used some research by W E B DuBois in her history paper.

_____ **8.** My mother works for Harcourt General, Inc, at their office in Florida.

_____ **9.** The George C Marshall Space Flight Center, a NASA facility, is located in Huntsville, Ala, which is north of Birmingham.

_____ **10.** I have an appointment with Mr Howard Meyers, Jr, at 2:00 P M.

EXERCISE B   Insert commas where they are needed in the following sentences. If a sentence does not require additional commas, write *C* on the line provided.

EXAMPLE _____ **1.** Michi, Susan, and I use various remedies for insomnia.

_____ **1.** When she can't get to sleep, Michi takes a relaxing bath drinks warm milk or reads a telephone book.

_____ **2.** To fall asleep quickly, Susan requires three things: fresh air and soft music and complete darkness.

_____ **3.** I visualize something that is quiet pleasant and peaceful.

_____ **4.** I often imagine that I am an astronaut touring the vast universe an explorer all alone in the silence of a huge forest or a biologist quietly enjoying the beauty of nature.

_____ **5.** I grow weary my eyes close and I fall asleep, undisturbed by blaring television sets loud ambulance sirens or noisy traffic.

Elements of Literature

WORKSHEET 3 | **Using Commas (Rules 12 g–k)**

EXERCISE A   Insert commas where they are needed in the following sentences. If a sentence is already correct, write *C* on the line provided.

EXAMPLES _____ **1.** The campers huddled around a bright**,** crackling fire.

_____*C*_____ **2.** Lucia likes fresh orange juice with her breakfast.

_____ **1.** Nishi groaned when she was jarred awake by the loud insistent sound of her alarm clock.

_____ **2.** The man wearing the red and white tie not the man in overalls is the owner of the bike shop.

_____ **3.** *Saifun* noodles are shiny thin transparent noodles often used in Chinese cooking.

_____ **4.** Brian is a warm honest person and I am glad to have him as a friend.

_____ **5.** Mike please pass me one of those delicious blueberry muffins.

_____ **6.** The trees on the Great Smoky Mountains help create a dense humid atmosphere which looks like a smoky mist.

_____ **7.** The Inland Sea is dotted by hundreds of hilly wooded islands.

_____ **8.** Jill brought chilled avocado soup a Caribbean dish to the International Club dinner.

_____ **9.** Yes a cold crisp salad with a sweet-and-sour dressing would taste good on a hot muggy day like this.

_____ **10.** At the Seattle Aquarium visitors can look through an underwater viewing dome to observe the marine life of Puget Sound.

EXERCISE B   Insert commas where they are needed in the following sentences. Do not be misled by compound verbs. If a sentence does not require commas, write *C* on the line provided.

EXAMPLE _____ **1.** We will read several haiku in class**,** and then we will write some of our own.

_____ **1.** I had not heard of Pat Mora before but yesterday I read her poem "Legal Alien."

_____ **2.** Our small vessel weathered every storm and brought us safely into port.

_____ **3.** Most of us found the movie dull but Abby liked it.

_____ **4.** The crowd swarmed onto the field and carried off the goal posts.

_____ **5.** Many Cajun families live by fishing and trapping but others farm or run businesses.

LANGUAGE HANDBOOK **12** **PUNCTUATION**

| WORSHEET 4 | Using Commas with Nonessential or Introductory Phrases and Clauses (Rules 12 i, j)

EXERCISE A   Insert commas where they are needed in the following sentences. If a sentence is already correct, write *C* on the line provided.

EXAMPLES _____ **1.** Samantha, who has always loved dogs, hopes to become a groomer.

_____C_____ **2.** The woman riding the white horse is Tina's aunt.

_____ **1.** The buildings that suffered the worst damage in the fire had to be torn down.

_____ **2.** Our YMCA facility which was built in the 1950s is undergoing remodeling and repairs.

_____ **3.** My brother attends Warm Springs Middle School which has an enrollment of 541.

_____ **4.** Congressman Sherman hoping for a compromise arranged a meeting with the president.

_____ **5.** Everyone who purchases at least two CDs will receive a free cap with the store's logo on it.

_____ **6.** Indonesian gamelan music is noted for orchestras consisting of drums, gongs, and xylophones.

_____ **7.** Gregor Mendel known for his experiments with garden peas formulated the basic laws of heredity.

_____ **8.** Some of the drama that was written during the reign of King Charles I is called "Caroline drama."

_____ **9.** The gold kitten which is very playful is the one I would like to adopt.

_____ **10.** The Prado which contains one of the world's finest art collections is the best-known museum in Spain.

EXERCISE B   Proofread the following sentences for the correct use of commas. Insert commas where they are needed, and draw a delete mark (⌐) through unnecessary commas. If a sentence is correct, write *C* on the line provided.

EXAMPLES _____ **1.** Students,⌐who write a third book report,⌐will receive extra credit points.

_____ **2.** The children, excited about their field trip, could not seem to keep quiet.

_____ **1.** Cricket is an English game that is played with bats and a ball.

Continued ☞

_____ **2.** All students, participating in the assembly, will be excused from class at 2:00 P. M.

_____ **3.** Mr. Wortham, trying not to chuckle, offered to help us clean up the mess.

_____ **4.** Romana Acosta Banuelos who was U.S. treasurer from 1971 to 1974 was the first Mexican American woman to hold such a high government post.

_____ **5.** Dorothy Crowfoot Hodgkin who won a 1964 Nobel Prize determined the molecular structure of vitamin B_{12}.

_____ **6.** Species of turtles, that live in regions with harsh winters, must hibernate.

_____ **7.** Ashley's family went to an exposition sponsored by the Zuni Cultural Arts Council.

_____ **8.** Speleologists are scientists, who study caves and the organisms that live in them.

_____ **9.** The puppy excited to see its owner wagged its tail vigorously.

_____ **10.** The word *volcano* comes from the word *Vulcan* which is the name of the ancient Roman god of fire.

EXERCISE C Insert commas where they are needed in the following sentences.

> **EXAMPLE 1.** Because she practices diligently, Carlota is becoming a much better tennis player.

1. Since water is deeper than it looks good spear fishers aim below rather than at their apparent targets.

2. If a fish underwater sees you on a pier you probably look as though you are higher than you really are.

3. By explaining the refraction of light through water I can give sensible reasons for these strange appearances.

4. Ascending the tree one branch at a time Mrs. Weinberg eventually reached the stranded kitten.

5. While I was working at the gas station I learned a lot about cars.

6. In the Cheyenne myth of the world's beginnings the coot and the turtle help create the land.

7. Chasing a fly ball in center field Armand stepped in a hole and sprained his ankle.

8. Angered by her brother's remarks Jan stamped out of the room.

9. As captain of the women's basketball team Lynette Woodard won an Olympic gold medal in 1984.

10. If people object to my suggestion let them state their reasons.

LANGUAGE
HANDBOOK **12** **PUNCTUATION**

WORKSHEET 5 | **Using Commas after Introductory Elements, and for Elements That Interrupt a Sentence (Rules 12 j, k)**

EXERCISE A   Insert commas where they are needed in the following sentences. If a sentence does not require commas, write *C* on the line provided.

EXAMPLE _____ **1.** Next, I would like to discuss the effects of air pressure changes.

_____ **1.** Yes air pressure can be tremendously important.

_____ **2.** Does a pressure cooker have a safety valve Clara?

_____ **3.** Changes in pressure can be quite dangerous.

_____ **4.** Oh then you know about the problems faced by divers.

_____ **5.** Yes flyers experience relatively slow changes in pressure compared to divers.

_____ **6.** One of the first places a diver feels pressure changes Teresa is the eardrum.

_____ **7.** I've heard Clara that divers hold their noses and blow when they start to feel pain in their ears.

_____ **8.** Yes swallowing also helps to equalize pressure.

_____ **9.** Why is it better for a diver to have perfect teeth than teeth with fillings Teresa?

_____ **10.** Air pressure exerts a different amount of force on the filling than on the tooth, and Clara under severe conditions it can cause a tooth to collapse.

EXERCISE B   Insert commas where they are needed in the following sentences.

EXAMPLE **1.** Yes, in late January a series of arctic blasts hit Europe and the United States and set new records for all-time low temperatures.

1. Oh I know the definition of *esprit de corps* a French phrase meaning "team spirit."

2. In your class Ms. Melton I have learned that an explanatory paragraph has more than one sentence, develops a central idea, and presents specific details.

3. On Saturday Angelo Santi our best trumpet player marched with the school band at the game in the afternoon and played in a dance orchestra at night.

4. No this machine a recent model does not use as much electricity, oil, and water as the older models.

5. School alterations a large item in the budget are necessary because of the inadequate cafeteria facilities and the undersized auditorium.

LANGUAGE HANDBOOK 12 PUNCTUATION

| WORSHEET 6 | **Setting Off Appositives with Commas (Rule 12 k)** |

EXERCISE A   Insert commas where they are needed in the following sentences.

> **EXAMPLE** **1.** *The Birds,* one of Hitchcock's most famous films, was released in 1963.

1. When Alfred Hitchcock the well-known director died in 1980, people mourned the loss of this master of suspense.

2. In one movie *Strangers on a Train* an innocent man becomes involved in a bizarre murder plot.

3. The climax of this movie a scene at a carousel thrills audiences.

4. Two things clever plots and unusual camera angles always add surprises to any Hitchcock film.

5. Hitchcock frequently used two devices the chase and the case of mistaken identity to build suspense in his films.

6. He didn't always write his own stories but sometimes based his movies on books such as *Rebecca* the romantic suspense story by Daphne du Maurier.

7. Who can forget the scene in *Rebecca* in which Mrs. Danvers the sinister housekeeper stands in the bedroom, engulfed in flames?

8. Hitchcock's peers other members of the film community admired both his talent and his sense of humor.

9. A number of directors have used "the MacGuffin" his method of using seemingly unrelated plot elements to set a story in motion.

10. One Hitchcock movie *North by Northwest* remains a classic the norm against which many similar movies of suspense are measured.

EXERCISE B   Combine each of the following pairs of sentences by taking a group of words from the second sentence and inserting it into the first sentence as an appositive phrase. Insert commas where they are needed.

> **EXAMPLE** **1.** The entire truckload spilled onto the middle of Halleck Turnpike. The truckload consisted of four tons of gravel.
> *The entire truckload, four tons of gravel, spilled onto the*
> *middle of Halleck Turnpike.*

1. My brother is reading "Osebo's Drum." It is an African folk tale. _____

_____

_____

Continued ☞

2. Ike blew the fuses again. He is one of our scientific geniuses. _____

_____

_____

3. Mrs. Nevins discovered the cause of the million-dollar blaze. She is the chief of the fire department. _____

_____

_____

4. I am working on Unit Five. The title of the unit is "The Westward Movement." _____

_____

_____

5. I saw Judy on the train. Judy is my cousin. _____

_____

_____

6. The class read *The Frontiers of Love.* It is a collection of poems by Diana Chang. _____

_____

_____

7. The house was built in 1860. It is an ornate mansion. _____

_____

_____

8. Mr. Ahmed asked us to ride in the plane. It was a tiny Piper Cub. _____

_____

_____

9. Do you remember Sue? She is the girl I told you about. _____

_____

_____

10. Aunt Alma arrived on Friday and asked Mom to accept a job in Portland. It was the day after Thanksgiving. _____

_____

_____

LANGUAGE HANDBOOK 12 PUNCTUATION

WORKSHEET 7 Using Commas for Parenthetical Expressions and for Dates and Addresses (Rules 12 k, l)

EXERCISE A Insert commas where they are needed in the following sentences.

> **EXAMPLE 1.** A person's attitude toward snakes, it seems, is largely determined by the person's culture.

1. Most people in the Western world in my opinion have an intrinsic dislike of snakes.
2. Westerners in fact use the expression "a snake in the grass" to describe a treacherous person.
3. However in many Eastern cultures the snake is revered.
4. Hindus for example have deep respect for the snake.
5. Generally speaking they see snakes as protecting rather than harming humans.

EXERCISE B Insert commas where they are needed in the following sentences.

> **EXAMPLE 1.** On January 5, 1998, Aunt Sabrina became director of human resources at a large company in Atlanta, Georgia.

1. On August 30 1997, you may have seen the New York Liberty play the Houston Comets in the first WNBA championship game.
2. Jan wrote to the General Electric Company Schenectady New York to obtain information about fluorescent light bulbs.
3. Mr. Van Dunk may be reached at 1120 Four Brooks Road Stamford Connecticut 06903, or at 420 Main Street White Plains New York 10601.
4. The letter addressed to 1425 Ocean Drive Long Beach, was forwarded to Tucson Arizona after a delay of several days.
5. The letter from Springfield Illinois was dated December 1 1998.
6. On August 28 1963, Dr. Martin Luther King Jr. spoke before a crowd of a quarter of a million people in Washington D.C.
7. Dear Al

   Just a note to say we look forward to seeing you in August.

   Yours truly

   John

8. After June 16 2000, mail your book to Cactus Literary Services in Austin Texas.
9. When did New York New York begin construction of the base of the Statue of Liberty?
10. I wrote to my favorite author in care of his publisher, Dalkey Archive Press Illinois State University Normal IL 61790-4241.

WORKSHEET 8 | Using Semicolons and Colons (Rules 12 m–r)

EXERCISE A   Insert semicolons where they are needed in the following sentences.

> **EXAMPLE 1.** Amber, Lahela, and Trisha will ride with us**;** Patrick and
> Stephanie will meet us at the theater.

1. My mom is reading *Shadow and Act* it is a collection of essays by Ralph Ellison.

2. Chemical changes occur constantly in nature for instance, lightning causes a chemical change in the air.

3. There are about fifty-five species of side-necked turtles they live in Africa, Australia, and South America.

4. The largest urban areas in Southeast Asia are centered around the cities of Manila, Philippines Jakarta, Indonesia and Bangkok, Thailand.

5. Ships on the Caribbean Sea might carry sugar from the West Indies coffee from Colombia, Costa Rica, or Guatemala or bananas from Panama.

6. The art of Africa has influenced art in other parts of the world for example, traditional African sculpture influenced the Spanish artist Pablo Picasso.

7. The Abeita family has three dogs, a cat, and a parrot and Jaime, Miguel, and Julia have been asking for a horse.

8. The boxer is a medium-sized, stocky, muscular dog it was named for its playful habit of striking out with its front legs.

9. The reviewer praised the special effects however, she criticized the screenplay.

10. The Navajo make up the second-largest group of American Indians in the United States only the Cherokee have more members.

EXERCISE B   Insert colons and semicolons where they are needed in the following sentences.

> **EXAMPLE 1.** Jim was supposed to meet me at 7**:**00**;** however, he did
> not show up until 7**:**15.

1. The letter began, "Dear Dr. Garcia Thank you for considering my application for kennel attendant at your clinic."

2. Katrina wrote her book report on *The Golden Gate A Novel in Verse* by Vikram Seth.

3. The play doesn't start until 8 00 P.M. however, we should plan to arrive early.

4. The lecture begins at 2 00 Dr. Durand will be discussing the literary elements of Psalm 104 1–50.

5. Mrs. Hershey has visited several cities in Canada Toronto, Ontario Edmonton, Alberta and Halifax, Nova Scotia.

| **WORSHEET 9** | **Test (Rules 12 a–r)** |

EXERCISE A   Insert end marks and commas where they are needed in the following sentences.

> **EXAMPLE 1.** Bonsai, the art of growing miniature trees, originated in
> China and Japan as early as the eleventh century A.D.

1. Marie Dorion an American Indian of the Iowa people was the only woman on the Astor Overland Expedition of 1811–1812

2. Oh what an exciting time we had on our white-water rafting trip

3. Always wear a helmet when you ride your bike and do not ride on busy streets

4. What is the elevation of Santa Fe New Mexico

5. Has Mr Kenneth C Hilbert who agreed to speak at the assembly arrived yet

6. Robin has moved to 1116 Mockingbird Blvd Savannah GA 31401

7. Lionel turn that radio down right now

8. The meeting of the Crestview Neighborhood Assoc begins at 11:00 A M and the topic will be crime prevention

9. Following the recipe carefully Theo made empanadas to serve at the party

10. Will you be able to meet me outside the library at 4:00 P M

EXERCISE B   Insert commas where they are needed in the following paragraphs.

> **EXAMPLE** [1] In the first half of the 1980s, Western wear, the
> traditional clothes of the cowhand, became high fashion.

[1] Yes boots dungarees and hats appeared on city streets as well as on the Texas plains. [2] Outfitted from head to toe city slickers it seemed had taken to wearing clothes from the American West. [3] Some bought the clothes brand-new "weathered" them until they looked appropriately worn and then treated them with care! [4] Others searched through used clothing stores garage sales and catalogs for "gently worn" items that more accurately reflected the fabrics buttons and trims of the real West; in fact from the moment they bought these clothes people treated their authentic Western wear with respect.

[5] Offered in a wide range of styles Western boots became very popular; many people had their boots custom made and some pairs definitely reflected individual tastes.

Continued ☞

[6] Toes could be rounded squared or needle sharp; heels too came in a variety of styles.

[7] Although dungarees were originally designed for cowhands miners and farmers the pants serve a more fashionable purpose today. [8] In nearly every town in the country people from all walks of life now wear these comfortable durable pants.

[9] Do you ever wonder about the widespread interest in the style shape and color of cowboy hats? [10] While the hat was orginally intended to keep sun rain sleet and snow off the cowboy's head the cowboy also used the hat to fan campfires to move the cows along or to hold a drink of cool water.

EXERCISE C   Insert semicolons, colons, and commas where they are needed in the following sentences.

> EXAMPLE **1.** Harris was distracted by all the noises outside**:** barking dogs**,** screaming children**,** and roaring car engines.

1. At about 10 45 the minister ended the Sunday school lesson with a reading of Proverbs 3 13.

2. Blaming severe snowstorms in Chicago for the delay the agent announced that the 6 30 flight would be two hours late.

3. In the basket were several different kinds of fruit bananas apples oranges and pears.

4. Aunt Linda Uncle Mike and Marcia arrived right on time but their luggage had been lost.

5. Trenell wanted to learn more about the Harlem Renaissance therefore he chose to write his biographical report on James Weldon Johnson.

6. We prepared for the camping trip by gathering several items cooking equipment sleeping bags hiking boots and other gear.

7. The Epsteins have moved many times they have lived in Dallas Texas San Francisco California and Billings Montana.

8. Beginning class promptly at 9 40 Ms. Lopez asked us to turn in our homework after she stacked our papers on her desk she began the class discussion.

9. Mother quoted Ruth 1 16 it is one of her favorite Bible verses.

10. I spent the afternoon at Bianca's house and she introduced me to the music of Bob Marley who was an important reggae artist.

LANGUAGE HANDBOOK 13 PUNCTUATION

WORKSHEET 1 | Italics and Quotation Marks (Rules 13 a, b, j)

EXERCISE A   In the following sentences, underline each word or group of words that should be in italics.

> **EXAMPLE 1.** The chorus will sing several songs from the Broadway musical <u>Ain't Misbehavin'</u>.

1. If I had to describe my cat in one word, that word would be independent.

2. I tried a Cuban dish that, in Spanish, is known as plátanos verdes.

3. The Japanese American newspaper Rafu Shimpo was founded in 1903.

4. The art professor was discussing I and the Village, a painting by Marc Chagall.

5. Natalie Merchant's CD Tigerlily, released in 1995, achieved platinum status.

6. My friend Annette is a big fan of the TV series The X-Files.

7. The s on that plaque is so ornate that it almost looks like an 8.

8. Jordan left out the second e when he spelled temperament.

9. The Phoenix was the first steamboat to make an ocean voyage.

10. In November 1982, the space shuttle Columbia made the first commercial satellite launch.

EXERCISE B   In each of the following sentences, underline the words that should be in italics, and insert quotation marks where needed.

> **EXAMPLE 1.** Eugenia Collier's short story "Marigolds" was first published in <u>Negro Digest</u> in 1969.

1. I was moved by Gary's expressive reading of Nani, a poem by Alberto Ríos.

2. The French word fleur-de-lis is sometimes used to refer to the iris.

3. The characters in James Baldwin's short story The Rockpile also appear in his novel Go Tell It on the Mountain.

4. Baby Blues was the title of last night's episode of the show.

5. Sakima was very proud of his essay, The Human–Animal Bond.

6. The CD Firecracker contains two of Jen's favorite Lisa Loeb songs, I Do and Truthfully.

7. Some concepts in the chapter Atoms and Molecules are difficult to understand.

8. Is the column For the Record a regular feature in the Sunday paper?

9. Isn't the song Evergreen from the motion picture A Star Is Born?

10. Jason found the fascinating article Brothers in Arms in a 1998 issue of American Legacy magazine.

LANGUAGE HANDBOOK **13** PUNCTUATION

| WORKSHEET 2 | **Punctuating Quotations; Using Quotation Marks to Enclose Titles (Rules 13 c–f, i, j)**

EXERCISE A Insert quotation marks, single quotation marks, and other marks of punctuation as needed in the following sentences. If a sentence is already correct, write *C* on the line provided.

EXAMPLES _____ 1. "Are you going to audition for a part in the play?" asked Julio.

___C___ 2. Dad told me I could watch TV if I finished the laundry first.

_____ 1. Did Ms. Uno really say Class, we will have the test on Friday asked Kim.

_____ 2. Miles Davis Chet announced is Aunt Marlene's favorite jazz artist of all time.

_____ 3. These tomatoes look ripe Waneta said Let's use them in the salad.

_____ 4. Howard said We're going to the movies. Do you want to go along

_____ 5. I just finished reading *House Made of Dawn* Michelle announced What a wonderful book!

_____ 6. Kara said that she did lots of hiking while on vacation in Colorado.

_____ 7. Discuss the following elements of the short story Conquistador: foreshadowing, flashback, and suspense.

_____ 8. The instructor reminded the boaters that life jackets must be worn at all times.

_____ 9. I think Dionne said We'll meet you at the soccer field a half hour before practice, Jiro said.

_____ 10. Have you seen any films by Satyajit Ray Elaine asked.

EXERCISE B On the lines provided, rewrite each of the following sentences, correcting all errors in punctuation and capitalization.

EXAMPLE 1. "Is it true Lena asked That bullfrogs are protected by law in some states"

"Is it true," Lena asked, "that bullfrogs are protected by law in some states?"

1. "In the southern Andes" the narrator continued. "Glaciers have cut deep valleys into the rocky coastline. _____

_____

2. "Heather's favorite poem is The Girl Who Loved the Sky; she has most of it memorized." _____

_____

Continued ☞

Elements of Literature

3. Then the director commanded everyone take your places! Jean said. _____
_____

4. Cliff Palace has many underground rooms called kivas the tour guide explained, the Pueblo people held their religious ceremonies in these rooms. _____
_____

5. Our band is going to play "La Bamba" in the talent show! exclaimed Shannon. _____
_____

6. "Wildflower gardens Mr. Brooks said can be inexpensive and easy to grow". _____
_____

7. "Would you like to go to the Lakers game with me, Tonya asked, I have an extra ticket.
_____

8. In her essay Marta focused on these aspects of the story Independence: theme, character, and tone. _____
_____

9. Randy said "The National Aquarium in Baltimore is so cool!" "Have you been there" ___
_____

10. "Then Shane sighed and said "I think we missed the bus." Todd said. _____
_____

EXERCISE C   Change each indirect quotation below to a direct quotation, and punctuate the new sentence correctly.

    EXAMPLE 1. I asked Tom to paint the trellis.
         "Tom, will you paint the trellis?" I asked. _____

1. Gabriella announced that she knew that Billy would apologize. _____
_____

2. Dad wondered where we were going and when we would return. _____
_____

3. I asked him if he would like to try using chopsticks. _____
_____

4. Jani shouted that she did not want to watch television. _____
_____

5. Shina asked me why I had not kept my promise to her. _____
_____

LANGUAGE HANDBOOK **13** PUNCTUATION

WORKSHEET 3 | **Punctuating Dialogue and Quoted Passages (Rules 13 c–h)**

EXERCISE A   Rewrite the following dialogue, using quotation marks, other marks of punctuation, and capitalization correctly. Remember to start a new paragraph each time the speaker changes.

EXAMPLE [1] What a beautiful white dog that is, Toni exclaimed, what breed is it. [2] This is an American Eskimo dog, Claudia replied. [3] Many people call them Eskies.

"*What a beautiful white dog that is!*" *Toni exclaimed.*
"*What breed is it?*"
      "*This is an American Eskimo dog,*" *Claudia replied.* "*Many people call them Eskies.*"

[1] With that thick, white coat, that dog must need lots of baths Toni said. [2] Actually, Claudia replied, This breed of dog is very clean. [3] Eskies have an oil on their fur that repels dirt, and they clean their paws and faces, much as a cat would. [4] That's really cool said Toni. [5] Are they smart [6] Oh, Claudia said. They're very intelligent and eager to please. [7] We've trained Juneau here to do quite a few tricks.

[8] Eskies sound like ideal dogs. said Toni. [9] What's the catch [10] Well, said Claudia, Juneau does need plenty of exercise and lots of attention, but he's definitely worth all the effort.

_____
_____
_____
_____
_____
_____
_____
_____
_____
_____
_____
_____
_____

Continued ☞

_____
_____
_____
_____
_____

EXERCISE B   Insert quotation marks and other marks of punctuation where they are needed in the following paragraphs.

> EXAMPLE   [1] "After reading this brochure," Ken said, "I'm interested in seeing these exhibits at the Houston Museum of Natural Science."

[1] The John P. McGovern Hall of the Americas opened in June of 1998 reads the brochure. [2] These exhibits focus on ancient civilizations in the Americas. [3] Visitors may follow the cultural story of the Western Hemisphere either chronologically or geographically.

[4] Examine the social, ritual, and spiritual activities of early North and South American cultures by studying the vast displays of photos, maps, toys, tools, and sculptures, encourages the brochure. [5] See re-creations of tepees, kivas, and other structures. [6] Learn about the survival methods of the Inuits, the Plains Indians, and the Hopis.

[7] In the Maya section, view astonishing masks and examples of recently deciphered writing, the brochure continues. [8] In the Aztec Gallery, enjoy the display of beautiful jars, cups, and pots, adorned with jaguars and feathered serpents.

[9] The Hall of the Americas is an exciting and educational experience for children and adults alike concludes the brochure. [10] You'll want to add it to your list of attractions to visit in Houston.

LANGUAGE HANDBOOK 13 PUNCTUATION

WORKSHEET 4 Test (Rules 13 a–j)

EXERCISE A Insert quotation marks, single quotation marks, and other marks of punctuation as needed in the following sentences. Underline any word or group of words that should be in italics. Circle each lowercase letter that should be capitalized.

> **EXAMPLE 1.** Mr. Nasumo asked, "(w)ho can describe the process of photosynthesis?"

1. I think said Jeremy that chorizo is the word for this spicy Spanish sausage.

2. Mr. Suarez said to me I will always have fond memories of the time I spent at the ranch, said Brandon.

3. Teresa tried to reassure me and said this too shall pass; but her words were of little comfort.

4. Are you familiar with the song Forever Your Girl, by Paula Abdul Kenesha asked.

5. Everyone appearing in Scene 2, Ms. Conlan said, please take the stage.

6. Mr. Feldman said look for the following elements as you read the poem American Hero: repetition, rhythm, and onomatopoeia.

7. This book Mrs. Mitchell said has a print of Three Flags, a painting by Jasper Johns.

8. This little girl may have a neck injury Jason warned don't move her until the medics have examined her.

9. For my birthday Rachel said my grandmother gave me the book Warrior Artists. It's about historic Cheyenne and Kiowa art.

10. As I placed the last brick in the wall, Fortunato cried for the love of God, Montresor

EXERCISE B Rewrite the following dialogue, using quotation marks, other marks of punctuation, and capitalization correctly. Remember to start a new paragraph each time the speaker changes.

> **EXAMPLE** [1] "Are you still working on that song" Jamie asked. [2] Well answered Gwen I want it to be just right.
>
> _"Are you still working on that song?" Jamie asked._
> _"Well," answered Gwen, "I want it to be just right."_

[1] So, what's the name of this new song of yours, anyway," asked Jamie. [2] I'm not sure Gwen answered, "right now I'm calling it "Snows of Minnesota," but that might not stick. [3] Jamie asked, is it really about snow. [4] The song actually is more about a state of

Continued ☞

mind," Gwen replied, snow is just one of the prominent images in the chorus. [5] If I can polish the lyrics just a little bit more, our band might be able to perform it in the fall talent show at school.

[6] That would be exciting said Jamie, what other songs are you going to play? [7] We're thinking about using Nat's song Pathways, and also another one of mine, called Daisy's Better Days. [8] I remember that one" Jamie said, "you played it at the party. [9] Well, I'll leave now so you can get back to work. [10] Okay, see you later said Gwen.

_____

_____

_____

_____

_____

_____

_____

_____

_____

_____

_____

_____

_____

_____

_____

_____

_____

_____

_____

_____

LANGUAGE HANDBOOK 14 PUNCTUATION

WORKSHEET 1 | **Forming Possessives with Apostrophes (Rules 14 a–b)**

EXERCISE   On the line provided, rewrite each of the following groups of words, inserting an apostrophe at the correct place to show possession.

EXAMPLES   _Bill's friends_   1. Bills friends

the dogs' tails   2. the dogs tails

_____   1. a friends family

_____   2. several friends families

_____   3. all the girls locker room

_____   4. Thomass hat

_____   5. two boys helmets

_____   6. the babys playpen

_____   7. Margaret Walkers poems

_____   8. the presidents speech

_____   9. both cars front bumpers

_____   10. one cars front bumper

_____   11. an employees welfare

_____   12. all employees welfare

_____   13. many trees branches

_____   14. a trees branches

_____   15. an officers uniform

_____   16. some officers uniforms

_____   17. Melissas brother

_____   18. Willies sister

_____   19. several voters opinions

_____   20. Mexicos history

_____   21. one fishs scales

_____   22. several fishs scales

_____   23. Frances countryside

_____   24. Charless book

_____   25. Mount Rainiers snow

LANGUAGE HANDBOOK **14** **PUNCTUATION**

WORSHEET 2 | **Using Apostrophes with Possessive Forms (Rules 14 a–f)**

EXERCISE A Most of the following sentences contain incorrect possessive forms. Draw a line through each error, and write the correct form on the line provided. If a sentence is already correct, write *C*.

EXAMPLES ___*Theirs*___ **1.** ~~Their's~~ is the best barbecue in Kansas City.

___*C*___ **2.** Josie found someone's softball mitt lying on the grass.

_____ **1.** This hat is too small for me; it's your's if you want it.

_____ **2.** Early in the season, we thought our team could win the championship.

_____ **3.** This dog should have it's teeth brushed every day.

_____ **4.** Both of the sculptures were appealing, but her's won the award.

_____ **5.** Someones castanets were found lying on the stage.

_____ **6.** "Do I have everyone's attention?" asked Mr. Sullivan.

_____ **7.** Both groups gave interesting demonstrations, but our's was more thorough than theirs.

_____ **8.** Willingness to listen to anothers ideas is a sign of maturity.

_____ **9.** We have finished our model already, and Shelly and Aaron will complete their's in time for the expo.

_____ **10.** Will anyone's presentation be on Mayan architecture?

EXERCISE B On the lines provided, revise each of the following items by using the possessive case.

EXAMPLE **1.** the guitar owned by Melissa and the one owned by Mark
Melissa's and Mark's guitars _____

1. one car belonging to Mom and Dad _____

_____

2. the team of Daphne and Jalene _____

_____

3. the house of her sister-in-law _____

_____

4. the mission of the Humane Society _____

_____

Continued 🖝

5. the umbrella owned by Danielle and the umbrella owned by Cody _____

_____

6. the daily specials of the Shoreline Cafe _____

_____

7. the books belonging to Phoebe and the books belonging to Todd _____

_____

8. the statement given by the attorney general _____

_____

9. the performance of the Ballet Folklorico _____

_____

10. the name tag of Rafael and the name tag of Robert _____

_____

EXERCISE C   Insert apostrophes where they are needed in the following paragraph.

> **EXAMPLE** [1] Jared's brother is fascinated by the escape artist Harry Houdini.

[1] Houdinis career had its beginning in the circus, where a few weeks work as an acrobat paid him only thirty-five cents per week. [2] Following his brother Theos departure from their act, Houdini launched the career that made him famous. [3] He always credited his joints ability to be dislocated and his diligent practice of the stunts and tricks as the keys to his success. [4] He was so adept at making objects disappear that his many critics closest inspections could not unmask his secrets. [5] Once he had learned how to make a 10,000-pound elephant disappear, he needed only several handlers aid and his own crews assistance to get the elephant on stage to begin the stunt.

LANGUAGE
HANDBOOK **14 PUNCTUATION**

WORKSHEET 3 Using Apostrophes, Hyphens, Dashes, and
Parentheses (Rules 14 c–h, j–o)

EXERCISE A Each of the following sentences contains at least one error in the use of
apostrophes or hyphens. Draw a line through each word that has an error, and write the
word correctly on the line provided.

> EXAMPLE 1. Mr. Sakata is always willing to listen to ~~anyones~~ opinion.
> _____*anyone's*_____

1. Although many nonChinese call the official language of China Mandarin, the Chinese
   prefer the term *putonghua*.

   _____

2. "Is this their lab equipment or our's?" asked Geraldo.

   _____

3. I chose foil backed wrapping paper for my origami figure, but Carol used a thin
   Japanese paper called *washi* for her's.

   _____

4. During her illness, Rebecca appreciated everybodys kind wishes and festively-wrapped
   gifts.

   _____

5. Risotto, a rice dish with vegetables, is a popular first course dish in Italy.

   _____

6. Andy's and Holly's wedding ceremony was the most beautiful one I'd ever attended.

   _____

7. Some peoples handwritten *A*s are so sloppy they look like *H*s.

   _____

8. Was Mrs. Shapiro complimentary of her new daughter's-in-laws first formal dinner?

   _____

9. After adding one half cup of milk, stir the mixture until it is smooth.

   _____

10. Both Chim and Leo's paintings make good use of color, but Chim's painting appeals to
    me more.

    _____

Continued ☞

EXERCISE B   Add hyphens, dashes, and parentheses where they are needed in the following sentences. (Do not add commas or colons.)

> **EXAMPLE 1.** Sharks are meat-eating fish (the most feared by humans) that live in oceans throughout the world.

1. The largest kind of shark the whale shark may grow up to 40 feet 12 meters long.

2. Whale sharks may weigh over 14 metric tons about the weight of three pickup trucks.

3. The smallest sharks are about 6 inches 16 centimeters long and weigh about 1 ounce 28 grams.

4. The fastest swimming sharks have a crescent shaped tail that is a powerful swimming aid.

5. A shark's teeth a shark has several rows of them are replaced often as older teeth fall out and new ones grow in.

6. Some people think that sharks must turn over on their backs in order to bite I know it's a myth.

7. Sharks hear very well only low pitched tones and listen for their prey.

8. Hammerhead sharks a group that includes a number of similar species are rather strange looking creatures.

9. Nurse sharks eat bottom dwelling fish as well as shellfish and sea urchins.

10. White sharks among the most dangerous sharks prey on large animals such as sea lions and tuna.

EXERCISE C   On the line provided, write the contracted form of each of the following items, using apostrophes to show where letters have been omitted.

> **EXAMPLE** _there's_ **1.** there is

_____	**1.** we have	_____	**11.** has not
_____	**2.** is not	_____	**12.** I will
_____	**3.** you are	_____	**13.** they are
_____	**4.** does not	_____	**14.** there is
_____	**5.** she will	_____	**15.** they will
_____	**6.** were not	_____	**16.** are not
_____	**7.** cannot	_____	**17.** who is
_____	**8.** he is	_____	**18.** you will
_____	**9.** do not	_____	**19.** it is
_____	**10.** let us	_____	**20.** will not

NAME _____ CLASS _____ DATE _____

LANGUAGE HANDBOOK **14** **PUNCTUATION**

WORKSHEET 4 | Hyphens, Dashes, and Parentheses (Rules 14 i–o)

EXERCISE A   On the lines provided, write each of the following words, adding hyphens to show where the word should be divided at the end of a line. Use a dictionary to check your work. If a word should not be divided, write *no hyphen*.

> **EXAMPLES** 1. preservation   *pres-er-va-tion*
>
> 2. aloof   *no hyphen*

1. tweezers _____
2. historic _____
3. through _____
4. chilling _____
5. determination _____

6. studious _____
7. buccaneer _____
8. domestic _____
9. longitude _____
10. monarchy _____

EXERCISE B   Each of the following sentences contains at least one word, pair of words, or prefix and a word that should be hyphenated. On the line provided, write each item that needs a hyphen, inserting the hyphen at the correct place.

> **EXAMPLE** *Twenty-four, week-long*   1. Twenty four of the software packages, about one third of the store's stock, remained after the week long sale.

_____ 1. This is a well made basket, but it does have one barely noticeable flaw.

_____ 2. The governor elect's speech was well received by most of the audience.

_____ 3. After scoring twenty one points in one game, Vanessa's confidence improved.

_____ 4. Marcia was pleased with her test scores, which ranked in the ninety second percentile.

_____ 5. The treasurer elect does not officially take office until mid March.

_____ 6. That museum has an extremely diverse collection of pre Columbian art.

_____ 7. A hush fell over the audience as the world famous soprano took the stage.

_____ 8. Ms. Ramirez, the president of the Environmental Council, is a well respected community leader.

_____ 9. The highly controversial bill passed by a two thirds majority.

_____ 10. After the first string quarterback was injured, the reserve quarterback saved the day.

Continued ☞

Copyright © by Holt, Rinehart and Winston. All rights reserved.

LANGUAGE HANDBOOK 14 WORKSHEET 4 *(continued)*

EXERCISE C Insert dashes or parentheses where they are needed in each of the following sentences.

EXAMPLES 1. Mr. Boylan ∧ my father, that is ∧ will be reading to us today.

2. Samuel Clemens (Mark Twain) wrote *The Adventures of Huckleberry Finn.*

1. "Mmm, I can't wait to taste that jambalaya as well as" Chad was saying just as the waiter approached our table.

2. Juan Sedillo 1902–1982 earned a Bronze Star Medal and five battle stars during World War II.

3. The Andes Mountains stretch along South America's west coast for a distance of 4,500 miles 7,200 kilometers.

4. The problem it's one that many athletes face is staying in top condition while not overtraining.

5. Wilma Rudolph did you know she had scarlet fever as a child? overcame many disadvantages to become an Olympic athlete.

6. Will Mrs. Wauneka I mean Dr. Wauneka be attending the conference next week?

7. Hokkaido see map on page 413 is the northernmost of Japan's four main islands.

8. My report the one for science class is on the formation of volcanoes.

9. Ms. Perkins visited four different states Nevada, Utah, Colorado, and Wyoming.

10. Mrs. Ebihari was a circuit court judge for sixteen years 1981–1997.

11. Do you think this monsoon season it seems to have arrived early will help the crops?

12. Our city's population it is growing is about 500,000.

13. Would you look at the new record set by our team in the mile I mean the meter relay!

14. The filament that fine piece of metal has burned in half in this light bulb.

15. Harriet exclaimed, "I don't know if I " and then fell silent.

16. Officer Tomkins has returned our tickets we lost them last night to Saturday's concert.

17. That wonderful old buckboard see its shiny, red wheels is leading the parade again this year.

18. Although Alfred attended college for four years 1993–1997, he has not yet graduated.

19. Columns plain steel, I believe will be added to the front of our school building.

20. Should we add Brussels sprouts to the shopping list it is getting pretty long?

LANGUAGE HANDBOOK **14** PUNCTUATION

WORKSHEET 5 Test (Rules 14 a–o)

EXERCISE A Insert apostrophes where they are needed in the following sentences.

> **EXAMPLE 1.** In my mother's office, some, of the books are hers and some of them are my father's.

1. "Theres one in every class," said Mr. Papas as Nick came in late without his notebook, textbook, or pencil.

2. Arnold Freiberg, the gray teams captain, tells me that hes confident of victory in tonights meet.

3. "No, Im afraid youre wrong about Dan," I said. "Its hard to get people to believe that he is nobodys fool."

4. In the Garcias back yard, the deers food is out in plain sight.

5. "If you read carefully," said Mrs. Chambers, "youll see that Whitmans and Frosts poetry have something in common."

6. At yesterdays track meet in Bloomfield, our opponents excelled in almost every event, but the final victory was ours.

7. After the coach diagrammed the play, his chalkboard was covered with *x*s and *o*s.

8. At Alans party we had Mrs. Kings potato salad, Mr. Bauers vegetable sticks, and Nancys fruit punch.

9. Dont try to touch Marcia and Rickys cat; its not fond of strangers.

10. The president-elects dog was featured on ABCs newscast last night.

EXERCISE B On the lines provided, write each of the following words, adding hyphens to show where the word should be divided at the end of a line. Use a dictionary to check your work. If a word should not be divided, write *no hyphen*.

> **EXAMPLES 1.** anticipation   *an-tici-pa-tion*
> **2.** enough   *no hyphen*

1. thrilling _____
2. mother-in-law _____
3. photograph _____
4. trust _____
5. chatter _____

6. involved _____
7. vigorous _____
8. Olympic _____
9. heartiness _____
10. amazed _____

Continued ☞

EXERCISE C   Insert hyphens, dashes, and parentheses where they are needed in the following passage. Do not use commas or colons.

> EXAMPLE 1. Our teacher ∧ Ms. Wong, I mean ∧ passed out twenty ∧ five copies of *The Red Badge of Courage,* by Stephen Crane (1871–1900).

1. Jonathan Crane Stephen's father was a Methodist minister; his mother was a strong minded advocate of moral behavior.

2. The main character of *The Red Badge of Courage* a young soldier named Henry Fleming survives a series of bone chilling events typical of combat.

3. Even though he wrote about the American Civil War 1861–1865, Crane was not born until 1871.

4. *The Red Badge of Courage* is his best known work; it and several of his short stories have been adapted to other media films, screenplays, and dramatizations.

5. Two of his stories "The Bride Comes to Yellow Sky" and "The Blue Hotel" were inspired by his trip to the American Southwest.

6. Crane lived for a while in Britain during the late Victorian era, and some of the best writers of the time H.G. Wells, Joseph Conrad, and Henry James became close friends of the twenty eight year old American.

7. While Crane was trying to cover a rebellion in Cuba Crane was also a journalist his ship sank, and Crane made it to shore in a small boat with three other men.

8. This near disaster was the basis of his greatest short story "The Open Boat."

9. Crane's early death he was only twenty eight when he died was the result of tuberculosis.

10. Stephen Crane was many different types of writer novelist, short-story writer, war correspondent, poet all rolled into one.

EXERCISE D   In the following paragraphs, underline each word that should have an apostrophe and write the word correctly in the space above.

> EXAMPLE [1] Underline(*People's*) <u>Peoples</u> dogs can be a constant source of entertainment.

[1] In one of Thomas Mertons stories, a visitor who likes dogs asks the owner what his dogs name is. [2] The owner, whos fond of playing practical jokes, promptly replies, "His names Rex." [3] Ive forgotten the dogs real name, but its certainly not Rex. [4] The visitors confusion grows when he cant get the dog to respond to any command. [5] Naturally, no self-respecting dogs going to do anything unless someone calls it by its own name!

LANGUAGE HANDBOOK 15 SPELLING

| WORKSHEET 1 | **Using Word Parts**

EXERCISE   On the line provided, divide each of the following words into parts (prefixes, roots, and suffixes), and write a definition based on the meanings of the parts. Check your definition in a dictionary.

EXAMPLE   **1.** psychic _psych|ic having to do with the mind_

1. microcopy _____

2. vision _____

3. overbuild _____

4. deportable _____

5. childish _____

6. rudely _____

7. politeness _____

8. chronic _____

9. hemisphere _____

10. biographer _____

11. interconnect _____

12. benediction _____

13. revert _____

14. actor _____

15. morphology _____

16. cyclist _____

17. phonic _____

18. tasteful _____

19. postgraduate _____

20. misjudge _____

21. untrue _____

22. multitude _____

23. discontinue _____

24. television _____

25. photograph _____

| WORSHEET 2 | Using Spelling Rules (Rules 15 a–c) |

EXERCISE A Fill in the blanks with the correct letters: *ie, ei, cede, ceed,* or *sede.*

> EXAMPLE 1. w_e i_rd

1. fr_____ght
2. suc_____
3. for_____gn
4. se_____
5. rel_____ve

6. inter_____
7. n_____gh
8. pro_____
9. th_____f
10. unv_____l

11. fr_____ndly
12. re_____
13. bel_____ve
14. _____ther
15. r_____gn

16. super_____
17. dec_____ve
18. con_____
19. p_____ce
20. h_____ght

EXERCISE B Some of the following sentences contain spelling errors involving the use of *ie, ei, cede, ceed,* and *sede.* For each sentence, underline the misspelled word and write it correctly on the line provided. If a sentence is already correct, write *C.*

> EXAMPLE ___ancient___ 1. The <u>anceint</u> Mound Builders lived in the Midwest and South.

_____ 1. What a great feeling to excede my own expectations for the pole vault and the mile relay!

_____ 2. You will receive extra points if you can list ten countries in Africa and can spell their names correctly.

_____ 3. Martha doesn't want to forfiet her place in line.

_____ 4. The Surpreme Court's latest vote superceeds last year's ruling on this issue by our state's court.

_____ 5. The cat's wieght goes up in the winter, when she stays inside more and gets less exercise.

_____ 6. My twin brother preceeded me in birth by just one minute, but he tells everyone he's my older brother.

_____ 7. Is it your beleif that term limits for officeholders are unconstitutional?

_____ 8. Janet's history report will be on Geronimo, the Apache cheif.

_____ 9. The government is willing to accede to the demands of its citizens if those demands are reasonable.

_____ 10. The veiw from Delphi was one of the many highlights of our two-week trip to Greece.

| **WORKSHEET 3** | **Adding Prefixes and Suffixes (Rules 15 d–j)** |

EXERCISE A   On the line provided, spell each of the following words with the given prefix or suffix.

EXAMPLE **1.** dry + ly = __*dryly*__

1. pure + ly = _____

2. engage + ment = _____

3. drip + ing = _____

4. re + enter = _____

5. day + ly = _____

6. breezy + er = _____

7. recur + ence = _____

8. cry + ing = _____

9. select + tion = _____

10. joy + ous = _____

11. im + material = _____

12. huge + est = _____

13. travel + ed = _____

14. brown + ness = _____

15. cheery + est = _____

16. hum + ed = _____

17. over + rule = _____

18. rope + ing = _____

19. happy + ness = _____

20. seventy + eth = _____

EXERCISE B   Some of the following sentences contain spelling errors involving the use of prefixes or suffixes. For each sentence, underline the misspelled word and write it correctly on the line provided. If a sentence is already correct, write *C*.

EXAMPLE __*trashiness*__   **1.** The yard's <u>trashyness</u> became impossible to tolerate any longer.

_____   **1.** Josh layed the magazines on the table and hurriedly left the room.

_____   **2.** Will the car get better milage when the carburetor is cleaned?

_____   **3.** "Too many oranges in this bag are overripe!" complained Harold.

_____   **4.** The merryment went on all evening during Cinco de Mayo.

_____   **5.** "The gently slopeing hills are perfect for beginning skiers," the instructor said.

_____   **6.** The audience wondered which of the two finalists would mispell a word first.

_____   **7.** The courageous man did not want any thanks or special attention.

_____   **8.** Rozanne went shoping for a sari, a garment worn by many women in southern Asia.

_____   **9.** Paul's gentlness is appreciated by everyone who knows him.

_____   **10.** My mother always says that one arguement usually leads to another.

LANGUAGE HANDBOOK **15** SPELLING

WORKSHEET 4 Forming Plurals of Nouns (Rules 15 k, l)

EXERCISE A On the line provided, spell the plural form of each of the following nouns.

EXAMPLE _halves_ **1.** half

_____ **1.** ratio
_____ **2.** sunburst
_____ **3.** dummy
_____ **4.** mouse
_____ **5.** cuff link
_____ **6.** ax
_____ **7.** phenomenon
_____ **8.** piano
_____ **9.** Kono
_____ **10.** holiday

_____ **11.** roof
_____ **12.** r
_____ **13.** Irish potato
_____ **14.** child
_____ **15.** calendar
_____ **16.** 9
_____ **17.** Murphy
_____ **18.** grass
_____ **19.** Japanese
_____ **20.** brother-in-law

EXERCISE B Some of the following sentences contain spelling errors involving the plurals of nouns. For each sentence, underline the misspelled word and write it correctly on the line provided. If a sentence is already correct, write *C.*

EXAMPLE _crises_ **1.** I admire people who remain calm in <u>crisis</u>.

_____ **1.** The lemurs from Madagascar seem to enjoy their new outdoor living area.

_____ **2.** The Rushs moved to Denver from El Paso about ten months ago.

_____ **3.** All the passerbys marveled at the work of the sidewalk artists.

_____ **4.** "Our taxs are actually lower now than they were two years ago," Mr. Carmichael said.

_____ **5.** The rainbow trout were beautiful in the clear spring water.

_____ **6.** The queen's lady-in-waitings numbered twenty-nine.

_____ **7.** Many people forget to dot their *i*'s when they write hurriedly.

_____ **8.** Several of the songes on the tapes were written by Scott Joplin, the famous ragtime composer.

_____ **9.** Do you still like to read the adventures of comic book superheros?

_____ **10.** Matt took care of the ponys on the ranch last summer.

Elements of Literature

LANGUAGE
HANDBOOK **15** SPELLING

WORKSHEET 5 | **Forming Plurals of Nouns (Rules 15 k, l)**

EXERCISE A   On the lines provided, spell the plural form of each of the following nouns and symbols.

EXAMPLE **1.** _women_ woman

_____ **1.** son-in-law   _____ **11.** cable

_____ **2.** Arapaho   _____ **12.** Sandy

_____ **3.** appendix   _____ **13.** Vietnamese

_____ **4.** key   _____ **14.** echo

_____ **5.** life   _____ **15.** shelf

_____ **6.** toll bridge   _____ **16.** stepmother

_____ **7.** rodeo   _____ **17.** class

_____ **8.** *to*   _____ **18.** #

_____ **9.** brush   _____ **19.** alto

_____ **10.** university   _____ **20.** goose

EXERCISE B   Some of the following sentences contain spelling errors involving the plurals of nouns. For each sentence, underline the misspelled word and write it correctly on the line provided. If a sentence is already correct, write *C*.

EXAMPLE _toys_ **1.** Adele's <u>toyes</u> are scattered all over the room.

_____ **1.** The lightning flashs were rather startling.

_____ **2.** The actions of the heroes will be noted by historians.

_____ **3.** Chinese lanterns were hung from the trees for the party.

_____ **4.** My uncles love to read mysterys.

_____ **5.** New maladys sometimes baffle doctors.

_____ **6.** Michael's tooths don't ache after his visits to the dentist.

_____ **7.** The Holidays recently returned from their own holiday in Trinidad.

_____ **8.** Supreme Court Justice Thurgood Marshall was one of her heros.

_____ **9.** For this test, count the number of *f*s in the sentence.

_____ **10.** The school newspaper has never had two editor in chiefs before.

LANGUAGE HANDBOOK	**15** SPELLING

WORSHEET 6 | **Test (Rules 15 a–l)**

EXERCISE A   Some of the following sentences contain errors in spelling. For each sentence, underline the misspelled word and write it correctly on the line provided. If a sentence is already correct, write *C*.

EXAMPLE   _slopped_   **1.** Joey <u>sloped</u> his soup out of the bowl.

_____   **1.** One feature of the couch I like is the interchangable cushions.

_____   **2.** Mr. Tims gave us two formulas to solve the problem.

_____   **3.** Would you intersede with the counselors on Mark's behalf?

_____   **4.** The cieling of the old Spanish mission was newly painted.

_____   **5.** The stereoes are on sale, but they're still too expensive.

_____   **6.** Two of our state's representatives intend to run for relection, and they probably will win.

_____   **7.** "I'm absolutely sure I can get all As on my report card," Eric said.

_____   **8.** Debbie has the most intricate dreadlocks in the whole school.

_____   **9.** Yogurt with bluesberries is my favorite afternoon snack.

_____   **10.** "You probably need to water the hollys more often," said Lisa.

EXERCISE B   The following paragraph contains ten spelling errors. Underline the misspelled words, and write each correctly on the lines provided.

EXAMPLE   [1] There's no <u>arguement</u>: cats are the most amazing pets.

1.   _argument_

[1] My three adventureous cats constantly astonish me and my new nieghbors in Little Italy. [2] The Siamese is one of the most capeable hunter's I've ever seen! [3] Of course, he has quick reflexs and sharp tooths. [4] All three cats apparently procede on the assumption that they are imortal. [5] They must have more than nine lifes because they surly go through that many daily.

1. _____   **6.** _____

2. _____   **7.** _____

3. _____   **8.** _____

4. _____   **9.** _____

5. _____   **10.** _____

Continued ☞

EXERCISE C   Some of the following sentences contain errors in spelling. For each sentence, underline the misspelled word and write it correctly on the line provided. If a sentence is already correct, write *C*.

EXAMPLE ___truly___ **1.** I <u>truely</u> enjoy watching basketball games.

_____ **1.** The choir joyfully entertained the bedridden children.

_____ **2.** My niece and two son-in-laws were born on August 15.

_____ **3.** "Okay, I conceed that I don't want to pick blackberries," Marta said.

_____ **4.** The ambassador was stuned by news of the invading armies.

_____ **5.** The Johnsons have superceded the McCoys on the guest list.

EXERCISE D   The following paragraphs contain ten spelling errors. Underline the misspelled word or words, and write the word or words correctly on the line provided. Not all sentences contain a spelling error.

EXAMPLE [1] Many <u>citys</u> celebrate Black History Month in February.

1. ___cities___

[1] The month is a special time to honor African American acheivements. [2] It also includes the birthdays of literary noteables Frederick Douglass and Langston Hughes. [3] Those knowledgable about the observance tell me it began in 1976. [4] They say,that the month-long observance was preceeded by a week-long celebration. [5] Negro History Week, begun in 1926, actualy led to Black History Month. [6] Credit is payed to Dr. Carter Godwin Woodson for starting Black History Month.

[7] Today, many communities receive As for their observances of Black History Month. [8] During this month, Kansas City, Missouri, celebrates its black heros. [9] The city boasts museum's honoring black pioneers and baseball players. [10] The music of legendary jazzmans Charlie Parker and Count Basie sets the city's tempo.

1. _____   **6.** _____

2. _____   **7.** _____

3. _____   **8.** _____

4. _____   **9.** _____

5. _____   **10.** _____

LANGUAGE HANDBOOK **16** **GLOSSARY OF USAGE**

WORKSHEET 1 **Common Usage Problems**

EXERCISE A Underline the word or expression in parentheses that is correct according to standard usage.

> **EXAMPLE 1.** (*Who's*, <u>*Whose*</u>) socks were left in the middle of the floor this morning?

1. After a short nap in the afternoon, Mom feels (*good, well*) and works until midnight.

2. The (*advice, advise*) from the captain was unexpected but most appreciated.

3. What is the (*morale, moral*) of this Alice Walker short story?

4. The new mower runs more quietly and cuts better (*than, then*) the old one.

5. If I had known you were coming, I (*would of, would have*) baked an apple pie.

6. "You were (*all together, altogether*) right about those boys!" Sue Lynn exclaimed.

7. The lowriders are (*kind of, rather*) impressive to see parading down the streets.

8. (*Fewer, Less*) entries in the contest were received this year.

9. (*Between, Among*) you and me, I think Patrick's idea is terrific.

10. I'm surprised that no one (*beside, besides*) Jason wants to learn how to sky-dive.

EXERCISE B Some of the following sentences contain errors in standard English usage. For each sentence, underline the error and then write the correct usage on the line provided. If a sentence is already correct, write *C*.

> **EXAMPLE** __*There*__ **1.** <u>Their</u> is a good chance of snow tomorrow.

_____ 1. People should think more about the principals by which they live.

_____ 2. The cellar was used to store food, tools, jars, and etc.

_____ 3. Chief Joseph gave his people and government officials wise council.

_____ 4. Sitting on the back row, we couldn't hardly hear the speaker.

_____ 5. What early people do you think discovered the wheelbarrow?

_____ 6. The incense doesn't smell bad to me, but it does to some others.

_____ 7. Like I said, igloos are most often dome-shaped.

_____ 8. Carl and Frieda said they will try to find a way to get to the party.

_____ 9. "Sit those packages down and give me a hug!" Aunt Irene said.

_____ 10. Martha couldn't find the right brand of spaghetti anywheres.

LANGUAGE HANDBOOK 16 GLOSSARY OF USAGE

| WORKSHEET 2 | **Common Usage Problems** |

EXERCISE A   Underline the word or expression in parentheses that is correct according to standard usage.

> **EXAMPLE 1.** (*Let*, *Leave*) us think about the right thing to do.

1. From her remarks during the talk, I (*implied, inferred*) that the speaker greatly admires Dr. Martin Luther King, Jr.

2. Our house is a long (*way, ways*) from here, on the far side of town.

3. The dog looks happy (*laying, lying*) on its side in the sun.

4. "The PBS show (*what, that*) I like best is coming on next," Earl said.

5. Julie did (*good, well*) on her speech about the history of potatoes.

6. My grandmother (*scarcely never, rarely*) makes her own tamales as she used to do.

7. It looks (*like, as if*) the debate team will go to the regional tournament for the first time in ten years.

8. We want to attend the concert in support of (*peace, piece*) in Northern Ireland.

9. Linda's hurtful words (*affected, effected*) my ability to concentrate.

10. The cat will surely find (*it's, its*) way home by tonight.

EXERCISE B   Most of the following sentences contain errors in usage. Underline the error, and then write the correct word on the line provided. If a sentence is already correct, write *C*.

> **EXAMPLE** __kinds__ **1.** Those <u>kind</u> of caps are warm and comfortable.

_____ **1.** Them persimmons are best eaten when they are completely ripe.

_____ **2.** People often startle theirselves when they discover their own hidden talents.

_____ **3.** Dr. Landers is the physician which helped my mother last year.

_____ **4.** Being as you've been to Guadalajara, tell us about the freeways in the interior of Mexico.

_____ **5.** The glass bowl busted when it fell from my hands and hit the floor.

_____ **6.** I gladly accept your invitation to the game.

_____ **7.** "I'll meet you outside of the auditorium at 7:00 P.M.," Adrian said.

_____ **8.** Spirituals they originated among African Americans in the 1700s.

_____ **9.** Jeff and I rose the banner above the doorway.

_____ **10.** Learn me to count to one hundred in Russian, please.

WORKSHEET 3 Test

EXERCISE A Underline the word or expression in parentheses that is correct according to standard usage.

> **EXAMPLE 1.** Did you remember to bring (*your*, *you're*) money?

1. "Please (*try to*, *try and*) see the situation from my point of view," Jerry said.

2. I admire Della Reese (*being as*, *because*) she is such an accomplished singer.

3. Rozanne (*implied*, *inferred*) that she will ask Mr. Vance about the problem.

4. The (*moral*, *morale*) of the story is to treat other people as you want to be treated.

5. Would you (*council*, *counsel*) me regarding my options for summer employment?

6. Chief (*Powhatan he*, *Powhatan*) was the father of Pocahontas.

7. Jane was tired and didn't feel (*good*, *well*), so she visited the doctor.

8. If Ned takes my (*advice*, *advise*), he will think seriously about his future.

9. The (*principal*, *principle*) sets the tone for the whole school, don't you think?

10. "When was the wheel (*invented*, *discovered*)?" remains an intriguing question.

EXERCISE B Most of the following sentences contain errors in usage. For each sentence, underline the error and then correct the error on the line provided. If a sentence is already correct, write *C.*

> **EXAMPLE** _might have_ **1.** You <u>might of</u> told me first about your plans to move.

_____ 1. Jean's French has improved some, but not enough for him to carry on a conversation.

_____ 2. I read in this brochure where artist Romare Bearden grew up in Harlem.

_____ 3. In my opinion, its a good article about the African American artist.

_____ 4. The vacation pictures aren't very clear, but they're all we have.

_____ 5. What kind of a soup do you intend to make for the potluck?

_____ 6. Your old dress shoes are actually shinier then your new ones!

_____ 7. Leave me tell you that a positive attitude is healthy for you.

_____ 8. A siesta is simply when a person naps.

_____ 9. We had only ten years of experience in sales among the five of us.

_____ 10. "It's okay to lie the packages on the table for now," Mother said.

Continued ☞

EXERCISE C   Underline the word or expression in parentheses that is correct according to standard usage.

> **EXAMPLE 1.** Isn't the library only a short (*ways*, <u>*way*</u>) down the road from your house?

1. (*Theirs, There's*) only one vegetarian entree on the menu.

2. Maybe she'll make it (*inside, inside of*) the building before the rain starts.

3. "That Buddhist shrine is (*all together, altogether*) lovely," Carla said.

4. We've seen (*fewer, less*) monarch butterflies pass through this year.

5. "(*Those, This*) kinds of games are childish and boring," said the boy.

6. (*Which, Who*) is the most stubborn person in our family?

7. The cat (*sat, set*) near the fireplace.

8. The actors didn't want to play the scene (*as, like*) the director had coached them.

9. They had not seen (*none, any*) of Steven Spielberg's movies.

10. Lorna gave Irene a large (*piece, peace*) of fabric for the community quilt.

EXERCISE D   Most of the following sentences contain errors in usage. For each sentence, underline the error and then correct the error on the line provided. If a sentence is correct, write *C*.

> **EXAMPLE** _____*accept*_____ **1.** Dad doesn't have to <u>except</u> the promotion, but he probably will.

_____ **1.** Reggae music always has an affect on me.

_____ **2.** When the ferret escaped from the house, where was Jonathan at?

_____ **3.** Many blows were necessary before the piñata busted open.

_____ **4.** Ms. Calaway will teach us to develop pictures tomorrow.

_____ **5.** Small food sculptures were made out of mushrooms, squash, celery, potatoes, and etc.

_____ **6.** For someone with little training, Jackie certainly works good in the office.

_____ **7.** Who besides Francois is eager to start the debate tournament?

_____ **8.** My singing may sound badly, but at least it is enthusiastic!

_____ **9.** All the students accept Matthew and Sheila wanted to postpone the test.

_____ **10.** "There is nowheres I'd like to work more than here," Angela said.